EMPOWERING RELATIONS AND SEX EDUCATION

The teaching of sex and relationships is now statutory, but many secondary schools and teachers are struggling with this essential topic. Can we really talk about sexual pleasure? How do we make our teaching LGBTQ+ inclusive? How do we engage boys with discussions about sexual violence? These and many other questions will be answered in *Empowering Relationships and Sex Education*.

This book helps schools understand that the statutory content is not the maximum they can do, rather it is the minimum they should do. Quality RSE offers young people skills for life. It empowers them to love themselves and find love with other people. It helps them acquire a clearer sense of themselves and their character and helps to develop empathy with others. It fosters a sense of agency and reciprocal sexual citizenship. It combats fear and shame around sex, unhelpful messages from porn, peer pressure and so much more. Good RSE is everything!

This book is a way for you to educate yourself on the many fascinating subject areas within RSE. It is a fantastic starting point for building a programme to meet student need and an essential resource for all RSE leads and teachers in secondary schools.

Jo Morgan (BA, PGCE, PGCert) is a multi-award-winning professional speaker, trainer and consultant. During her 15 years in teaching, she gained national attention and acclaim for her groundbreaking work on Relationships and Sex Education (RSE), LGBTQ+ inclusion and Wellbeing. Since then, she has been on a mission to spread the success of her initiatives to schools and universities across the UK and beyond. As the founder and CEO of Engendering Change, she leads a team of specialist consultants who, through inspirational training and community projects, empower individuals and organisations to rationalise and embrace a commitment to Equity, Diversity and Inclusion (EDI), and Wellbeing.

Access your Online Resources

Empowering Relationships and Sex Education is accompanied by a number of printable online materials, designed to ensure this resource best supports your professional needs

Go to https://resourcecentre.routledge.com/speechmark and click on the cover of this book

Answer the question prompt using your copy of the book to gain access to the online content.

EMPOWERING RELATIONSHIPS AND SEX EDUCATION

A Practical Guide for Secondary School Teachers

Jo Morgan

Routledge
Taylor & Francis Group

LONDON AND NEW YORK

Designed cover image: © Getty Images

First edition published 2024
by Routledge
4 Park Square, Milton Park, Abingdon, Oxon, OX14 4RN

and by Routledge
605 Third Avenue, New York, NY 10158

Routledge is an imprint of the Taylor & Francis Group, an informa business

British Library Cataloguing-in-Publication Data
A catalogue record for this book is available from the British Library

Library of Congress Cataloging-in-Publication Data
Names: Morgan, Jo (Sex education consultant), author.
Title: Empowering relationships and sex education : a practical guide for secondary
school teachers / Jo Morgan.
Description: First edition. | Abingdon, Oxon ; New York, NY : Routledge, 2024. |
Includes bibliographical references. | Summary: -- Provided by publisher.
Identifiers: LCCN 2023056922 (print) | LCCN 2023056923 (ebook) |
ISBN 9781032571263 (hardback) | ISBN 9781032571256 (paperback) |
ISBN 9781003437932 (ebook)
Subjects: LCSH: Sex instruction. | Sex instruction for teenagers. | Sex educators.
Classification: LCC HQ57.3 .M67 2024 (print) | LCC HQ57.3 (ebook) |
DDC 613.9071--dc23/eng/20231227
LC record available at https://lccn.loc.gov/2023056922
LC ebook record available at https://lccn.loc.gov/2023056923

ISBN: 978-1-032-57126-3 (hbk)
ISBN: 978-1-032-57125-6 (pbk)
ISBN: 978-1-003-43793-2 (ebk)

DOI: 10.4324/9781003437932

Typeset in Interstate
by Deanta Global Publishing Services, Chennai, India

Access the Support Material: https://resourcecentre.routledge.com/speechmark

To Mum & Dad, the original empowering sex educators.
Thank you for your honesty, openness and laughter.
You taught me to love myself and to channel my power to lift others up.
Sorry for being the ultimate rebel without a cause and for waiting until adulthood to realise how wise you both are.

With gratitude and love,
Jo

CONTENTS

PROLOGUE

I was taught sex education by a nun (we'll call her Sister Anne). Whilst Sister Anne undoubtedly did her best to deliver this content, the experience for all of us was pretty awkward. As students tried to embarrass her with inappropriate questions ("Are you still a virgin then, Sister Anne?") and stifle their giggles, a darker side began to emerge. The condemnation of homosexuality and, indeed, any sexuality outside of marriage left some feeling confused, ashamed and guilty. The censorship of contraception advice was also problematic. Few (if any) students managed to delay sex until their wedding night and were left ill-informed about how to keep themselves safe. The exclusive focus on the male ejaculate (and no mention of female sexual pleasure) left many girls expecting and accepting unpleasant and often painful sex.

But I was one of the lucky ones. My parents were always completely honest and open about sex. They encouraged my brother and me to be curious, ask questions and never feel a sense of shame or fear.

When I became a Religious Studies teacher, it hadn't occurred to me that I would later become an RSE teacher. However, when I was later promoted and became responsible for the personal, social, health and economic (PSHE) programme, I was shocked to discover how little the RSE content had improved since my experience as a child. Although this was not a faith school, the approach was exclusively heteronormative, focused entirely on risk reduction and had no mention of female sexual pleasure. I became utterly convinced that this failing had to be remedied immediately.

As I set about overhauling the curriculum, I was fortunate to work with a Head who fully supported me. I was given training, time, status and support to transform the mission and delivery of RSE. Increasingly, this work garnered national attention, and I was asked to share how this progress was achieved by speaking at conferences and schools across the country. In 2020, the Sex Ed Forum awarded me Best RSE Teacher (Secondary) in the UK, and in 2022 I left teaching to run my training and consultancy company Engendering Change full-time.

INTRODUCTION

Relationships and Sex Education (RSE) became statutory in September 2020. This move ensures that all English primary schools are required to teach Relationships Education and all secondary schools Relationships and Sex Education.

However, whilst the Department for Education (DfE) guidance was welcome, many experts felt that opportunities had been missed. Parents still have the right to withdraw their children from sex education (as long as it's not the Science content, up to three terms before the child's 16th birthday). Many essential topics like sexual pleasure, female sexuality, rape culture and pornography were given little or no mention. Faith schools are free to interpret the content from their religious perspectives and, whilst many faith schools are delivering good RSE, the provision across the country remains woefully inconsistent.

Teachers are nervous about RSE and the ambiguity in the guidance has not helped. RSE leads often find themselves given the role as an afterthought. They are rarely trained properly and struggle to find quality resources. Many schools use tutors to deliver the content, some of whom feel incredibly nervous about doing so. We have a deficit of time, training and subject knowledge, yet teaching RSE is a statutory requirement. At the same time, the same government that introduced statutory RSE has raised concerns about inappropriate content being taught, particularly by external providers. During Prime Minister's Questions in March 2023, Conservative MP Miriam Cates decried RSE as a "catastrophe for childhood," claiming that children are receiving "graphic lessons on oral sex, how to choke your partner safely, and 72 genders." Moral panic spread across social media, despite there being little to no evidence to substantiate these claims. When Rishi Sunak later announced an urgent review into RSE, experts in the field welcomed this but cautioned that such a review must be evidence led.

DOI: 10.4324/9781003437932-1

Against this difficult backdrop, this book aims to empower teachers with the rationale, evidence and practical strategies for delivering positive and impactful RSE. It will help teachers to ensure they are fully compliant with the statutory framework but also understand that this is not the maximum they can do, rather the minimum they should do.

Quality RSE is one of the greatest gifts schools can give to young people. It offers life skills that will help them to be healthy and happy whilst at school and as adults. It empowers them to love themselves and find love with other people. It helps them acquire a clearer sense of themselves and their character and helps them to develop empathy with others. It fosters a sense of agency and reciprocal sexual respect and fulfilment. It combats fear and shame around sex, unhelpful messages from porn, pressure to act in ways they are not happy with and so much more. Good RSE is everything!

This book is for all RSE leads and teachers in secondary schools. You will learn about the many fascinating subject areas within RSE and become empowered to plan and deliver outstanding lessons that will benefit your students for the rest of their lives.

A NOTE ON... Using this Book

Throughout this book you will find practical strategies for delivering RSE. These suggestions provide a starting point for building a programme to meet student need and are not designed as an off-the-shelf scheme of work. Every child, class and school will have different needs. It is, therefore, the responsibility of the RSE lead to ensure that the content is delivered in an age- and stage-appropriate manner. Regularly consulting students and parents, providing full transparency on your approach and remaining mindful of current trends will all help to ensure a bespoke, appropriate and evidence-led approach which supports the statutory framework.

1 Aims and Ethos

Often RSE programmes are cobbled together without giving any real thought to the aims and ethos underpinning the programme. Resources are inherited, subject leads are given very little time or training and so starting from scratch and reflecting on the school's approach to RSE rarely happens.

RSE leads understand that they need to teach everything on the statutory framework, but, other than risk reduction, there is often an absence of a clearly articulated philosophy to underpin the programme.

Working this out is a great place to start. It can help make sense of everything: why you teach what you teach, when you teach it, your approach in the lessons, the content of the curriculum and the students' outcomes.

This clear articulation can then become the ongoing thread which ties everything together. It empowers staff with a centrally agreed approach and a clear sense of the strategic intentions of RSE. It ensures that planning and delivery of lessons are structured with coherence and delivered consistently. It informs students and parents of the stance the school has taken and how this fits with the school's broader aims.

So, what should this look like?

This will depend on the context of your own school and the opportunities and limitations within this. The advice below may be adjusted according to whether you are in a faith school, the level of support you have from your senior leaders and your own position in the school.

Where to start:

DOI: 10.4324/9781003437932-2

1. Students: Rather than speaking to students and ascertaining their needs, schools often work on assumptions when it comes to RSE. Try creating a working group of students and ask them to help shape a clear picture of what they want to get from their RSE lessons. Combine this discursive process with anonymous student surveys and use this data to drive and justify decision making.

2. Parents: Schools are obliged by the Department for Education statutory guidance (2020) to meaningfully engage parents in the development of their RSE policy. This can be tricky, but it can also be a great opportunity to engage parents in the development of the programme and to create advocates for the school's provision within the parent body. If there is an incongruence with parents' views and their children's, as a school you can play a vital role in bridging this gap. Use this engagement as an opportunity to educate parents about what young people are saying. The statistics you have gathered from your student engagement will help to support the approach you are taking. Linking this to the aims and ethos of RSE and the broader school aims can help you to adopt a robust approach, whilst still building in flexibility. If parents express concern about a particular part of the curriculum, use this as an opportunity to educate the whole school community on this issue.

CASE STUDY

School X was made aware that some parents were making negative comments on a Year 9 parents' WhatsApp group about a lesson on identity. Following this, some Year 9 students began expressing intolerant views and bullying a transgender student. The school invited parents to an evening event on this subject. An external speaker delivered a workshop on sex, gender and sexuality and gave a talk on the Equality Act. The Head of RSE and Head Teacher showed the resources from the lesson in question and spoke about the school's aims and ethos for RSE. They discussed this in the context of the broader school aims and explained their desire to help all students to be happy, authentic and resilient to difference. They reassured parents that they were helping their children to acquire the skill of critical thinking, rather than pushing a particular stance or gender ideology. They invited parents to then follow up individually with any concerns. This event was well received, and no complaints followed.

A NOTE ON... **Parental Right to Withdraw**

Parents do not have the right to withdraw their child from relationships education at primary or secondary level.

A parent has the right to request that their child be withdrawn from some or all of the sex education which the school teaches as part of the RSE programme but not that covered by the statutory science curriculum. This parental right continues up to and until three terms before the child turns 16. After that point, if the child wishes to receive sex education, the school should make arrangements to provide it during one of those terms, including catch-up material.

It is a good idea to include the school's processes around this in the RSE Policy. For example, a school may state that:

1. Any request for withdrawal should be made in writing to the Head.

2. Before granting the request, the Head will discuss the request with parents and, as appropriate, with their child to ensure that their wishes are understood and to clarify the nature and purpose of the curriculum.

3. Right to withdraw is based on opt-out, rather than opt-in, and that an outline of the content will be published at the beginning of the academic year, rather than ahead of each RSE module.

There may be situations in which particular consideration needs to be given to a student's specific needs, such as those arising from trauma. Once those discussions have taken place, except in exceptional circumstances, the school should respect the parents' request to withdraw the child, up to and until three terms before the child turns 16.

If a child is withdrawn from sex education, this is likely to be for only a small part of a lesson as much of the RSE content is delivered in Science or in Relationships or Health Education. During such a period of withdrawal, a student should receive purposeful education (Department for Education, 2020).

3. Networks: It is also a good idea to find out what other schools in your local authority are doing. Where progress has been made in a similar school to yours, this comparison will be useful as you make the case for prioritising RSE to your senior leaders. Forming a support network with other subject leads can be useful for sharing resources, best practice, and recommendations on local training providers.

4. Articulating your aims and ethos: A clear articulation of this is essential to help guide your planning, delivery and communication regarding RSE. Whilst each school will want to create a bespoke version of this, the following pillars will help to create the most impactful RSE:

    a. An empowering approach. Students are empowered with knowledge and skills to make informed decisions about sex and relationships which are right for them.

    b. A positive approach. Sex and relationships are discussed in positive terms and scare/ fear tactics are avoided. Students understand that sex can be a beautiful and pleasurable thing when they and their partner(s) have the knowledge and skills to make decisions which are right for them.

TROUBLESHOOTING – A Note on Sex Positivity

There has been some controversy and misinformation around this term. Some have regarded sex positivity as the promotion of prom-iscuity and condemnation of abstinence; an approach which promotes unbri-dled freedom to engage in any sex act. Rather, sex positivity is about helping students to explore the positive, pleasurable aspects of sex rather than an exclusive focus on risk management and fear. It is about examining what healthy relationships might look like, rather than exclusively focusing on abu-sive relationships. It is about meeting students where they are, helping them to understand what the content means for them personally and thus ensure the greatest engagement and impact. If schools choose to use the term sex positive in their communication, it is important to include a clear definition to avoid unnecessary controversy. Alternatively, schools may choose to use 'empowering' or 'positive' as a catch-all term instead.

---

    c. A fully inclusive approach. Every student should see themselves represented in the curriculum. LGBTQ+ issues are not a one and done and should be embedded throughout. See Chapter 5 for further details.

    d. A student-led approach. In addition to starting a review of RSE by consulting students, this process should be repeated every year and the programme adapted accordingly. Rather than work off assumptions, it is essential that students lead the development of the curriculum to ensure it is constantly adapting to meet their needs.

CASE STUDY

School X had been seeking to improve its prevention of child-on-child sexual abuse and harassment. They invited students to work in small groups (single and mixed sex) to help inform what should be covered in the curriculum. Students reported that little attention had been given to the impact of sexual abuse. Following this, the school adapted their lesson plans to incorporate this. They encouraged students to identify potential short- and long-term impacts themselves and to create their own case studies. The teachers guided students to consider issues like trust, self-esteem, body image, sexual fulfilment and the law. When the school consulted students in the next annual review of RSE, they reported greater engagement with this topic and found the lessons more impactful.

e. A character-led approach. In combination with the PSHE programme, RSE should help students to acquire a keen sense of their own principles and values and understand how their attitudes and behaviours around relationships and sex are fundamental to this. Helping young people to understand their rights and responsibilities around sex is crucial and made possible when they properly engage with what each of the lessons means for them personally.

f. A non-judgemental approach. Students will have different backgrounds, faiths and values and this should be reflected in the curriculum and supported in the lessons. Students should be encouraged to reflect on the lens through which they view the world and understand the relevance of this as they engage with the topics. RSE is not without agenda. We have clear aims for our students to be sexually healthy, respectful and law abiding. However, there will be a vast range of perspectives and belief systems which our students will bring to the classroom.

A NOTE ON…Non-Judgement

Consider how a teacher's judgement could become apparent when discussing the following: anal sex, watching porn, having multiple partners, asexuality, religious views about sex and so on. Ask yourself how each of these examples could be discussed in a non-judgemental way.

g. An expert-led approach. It is essential that the staff delivering RSE have the knowledge, skills and willingness to do so effectively. Helping all staff to understand the agreed aims and ethos and empowering them with training and support is essential. Using expert external speakers is useful but maximise this opportunity by asking those experts to deliver staff training to all staff too. Students' experience of external sessions will be enhanced by their RSE lessons with highly skilled teachers who they know and trust and through topics which are delivered within the school, over a period of time.

TROUBLESHOOTING

Many teachers feel concerned that teaching RSE is personally exposing. To combat this, in Lesson 1 and every lesson, the same rule should be emphasised: Nothing personal. Make it clear that nothing is taboo in RSE lessons, except personal questions or declarations. (See further suggested ground rules in the Teacher Toolkit below.)

---

h. A consent-centred approach. The programme must help students understand boundaries, consent and the law, and how this relates to pleasure, relationships and their character. See Chapter 6 for more on this.

i. An adaptive and current approach. Trends around online behaviours, new risks and so on must form part of an annual review of the programme. Student engagement will help with this, but the RSE lead will also need regular training and engagement with new trends.

5. Support from senior leaders: Having your senior leaders onside is essential in making your RSE programme a success. Helping them to see the value in RSE and the need to prioritise this can be a challenge but the case for quality RSE is incredibly strong.

TROUBLESHOOTING

If your Senior Leaders are not supportive of committing to prioritising RSE, make the case:

- The Moral Case: We owe it to our students to provide them with excellent RSE. It is fundamentally crucial to their lives.

- The Business Case: Students' learning outcomes will be negatively impacted by a failure to deliver this. If a student is engaging in risky sexual behaviour / experiencing self-loathing or bullying about their sexuality / in an abusive relationship, etc., their ability to learn and perform in exams will likely be damaged.

- Preparing for inspection: Increasingly, school inspectors are examining RSE and expecting not just statutory compliance, but a whole-school approach towards issues like child-on-child sexual abuse and harassment.

- Delivering RSE is a statutory obligation.

- When done well, RSE will contribute to achieving many other school aims:

  ○ It acts as a useful preventative measure to certain safeguarding issues.

  ○ It helps to combat unhelpful and dangerous misinformation students may have been exposed to.

  ○ It promotes Character Education, Wellbeing and Health Education.

  ○ It has life-long relevance.

- Use the data gathered from your student engagement to demonstrate:

  ○ That students want RSE lessons.

  ○ That students need this intervention.

  ○ That many students' parents are not discussing these issues with them.

- Make the case for timetabled lessons and the use of passionate, expert staff.

- Make the case that leading RSE is a whole-school role, benefitting every student and should be given the time, pay, status and budget necessary.

- Use the Sex Ed Forum's *Relationships and Sex Education: The Evidence* (2020) to demonstrate the undeniably positive impact of RSE on so many student outcomes.

TEACHER TOOLKIT

Suggested Ground Rules

1. THIS IS THE MOST IMPORTANT RULE... Nothing personal. Don't ask anyone in the room a personal question. Don't make a personal comment about anyone (whether they're in the room or not), don't reveal anything personal about yourself.

2. Unless it breaks Rule Number 1 you can ask ANYTHING! Please ask lots of questions and come to class with questions.

3. It's okay to laugh!

4. If any of the content worries you, please let me know. If you need to chat, I'm here.

5. This is your opportunity to learn everything you can about sex. Make the most of it!

6. It's okay (and inevitable) that there will be differences of opinion in the class. Let's be positively curious and respectful.

7. We will explore which topics are going to be covered ahead of the lessons. If any aspect of this concerns you, or if you would like to have a chat first, please come and see me.

TROUBLESHOOTING – Should you really answer any question?

In short, yes. As long as Rule Number 1 (nothing personal) is respected, allowing students to ask anything is a great way to help them feel comfortable and to get any awkwardness out the way. If a teacher refuses to answer a question this is likely to undermine an empowering approach and lead students to find the answer from questionable sources. Even if a silly question is asked with the intention of causing laughter, this can be a great way to break the ice. Once students see their teacher is unphased and that laughter is okay, they will soon move on to wanting to find out as much as they possibly can. If you don't know the answer to a question, don't be afraid to say so. Promise you'll find out and report back next lesson (don't make the mistake of Googling the question in front of the class as you may end up with some unfortunate answers displayed on your screen).

Anonymous questions can be great fun and useful, particularly if you are short on time. However, ultimately, helping students to discuss sex openly and to ask questions in this safe space will build their sexual literacy.

A NOTE ON... Sexual Literacy

'Sexual literacy' refers to an individual's ability to talk openly about sex in an appropriate and healthy manner. For example, engaging in a discussion in an RSE lesson, speaking to a health care professional about contraception choices or reporting an incident of sexual violence. A key benefit of RSE is to help students to acquire the skill of sexual literacy. This theme will be revisited throughout the book.

TEACHER TOOLKIT

Setting the Tone Activity - Lesson 1

At the beginning of every RSE topic, the following activity can be repeated.

Explain: sex is a big part of life for most people. Good sex can contribute positively to a person's wellbeing, mental health, feelings of safety and security, pleasure, intimacy and so much more. Bad sex can do the very opposite - it can damage a person's wellbeing and mental health, it can make people feel insecure and unsafe, it can be devoid of pleasure and intimacy.

Issue groups with blank A3 paper and ask them to draw a line down the middle and write 'good sex' on one side and 'bad sex' on the other.

Ask groups to discuss and add ideas around good and bad sex (features and impact). Encourage them to think about physical and mental considerations. Seek feedback and discuss as a whole class. This is a great ice-breaker and the students will begin to see that there is no taboo here. Invite discussions about what kinds of things might contribute to the positive and negative sides of sex and relationships. Encourage them to reflect on what they want for themselves and for their future partners. This should be led by the students with you acting as a facilitator, drawing out ideas like consent and respect and challenging where appropriate.

These open discussions about the positive aspects of relationships will help them begin to understand what positive sex looks like. This can help to challenge narratives in porn, myths about sex and inequitable attitudes towards sexual pleasure. The aim is to help them develop the skills of self-reflection, effective communication and empathy with others.

Explain: Of course good/bad sex are subjective concepts. However, common agreement is often found on some of the features of 'good sex' like trust, orgasms, pleasure, fulfilment, happiness, intimacy, etc., and bad sex, e.g., abusive, painful, lacking consent, no pleasure. During this topic we will be investigating how to tip the scales in the right direction for you and your future partner(s).

Sexual literacy:

Sexual literacy is one of the key skills you will acquire during this course.

Discuss:

1. What are the practical benefits of sexual literacy?

2. How might an absence of sexual literacy be problematic?

Will you challenge yourself to develop this skill as the course progresses?

Sexual literacy is knowledge of sexual health and wellbeing. It empowers us to access sexual health services, communicate about our needs and be more reflective about our sex lives. The absence of sexual literacy can be the source of many health and social hazards, including exposure to sexually transmitted infections (STIs), unwanted pregnancies, secrecy around sexual abuse and violence, an obstacle to sexual pleasure and much more.

Keep the sheets of paper and refer back to these in future lessons. Alternatively, take a photo of the version you have create on the white board from all their ideas and embed this in your slides for future lessons.

Positive Puberty:

When teaching Puberty lessons with Year 7 (or younger) students, students sometimes find that the lessons engender a sense of fear and disgust. Such an approach runs the risk of making students feel shame about their bodies, anxiety about the changes they will experience and poor self-esteem and body image.

Instead, a positive take on puberty can help students to feel more at peace and even happy about these changes.

Suggested strategies:

1. Ask students to create a mood board on their future selves, depicting their hopes and the things they are looking forward to. Encourage them to reflect on this as you explore the changes of puberty.

2. Use the power of laughter! Things like wet dreams, accidental erections, boobs and so on can be funny to discuss. Lean into this with students.

3. Students of all genders should be learning about periods. Pass a variety of sanitary products around the room. Ask them to think about what the pros and cons of each might be. Highlight where in the school these can be accessed and ensure there are multiple places where students can easily get these.

Ensuring Compliance with the Statutory Framework:

The framework is lengthy and can feel daunting, particularly when time allocated to RSE is limited. However, each element of the framework does not have to be taught as a discrete lesson. Indeed, it is possible to cover several elements within one lesson.

Use the table below to highlight where each of the elements is covered in your scheme of work.

It is also likely that many of the elements are already being taught in academic lessons. For example, reproduction and sexual health in Biology, families and marriage in Religious Studies and online risks in Computing.

Share the table below with other relevant Heads of Department and ask them to add where they cover each element.

This will help you to evidence your compliance and to spot, then cover, any gaps. You may also find that you are able to free up some of your curriculum time by avoiding repetition.

	The Department for Education (2020) Statutory Framework for RSE: Key Stage (KS) 3 and 4	
	Statutory Requirements: "Schools should continue to develop knowledge on topics specified for KS1/2 as required <u>and in addition</u> cover the following content by the end of KS4:"	**Evidence of coverage:**
Families	That there are different types of committed, stable relationships.	
	How these relationships might contribute to human happiness and their importance for bringing up children.	
	What marriage is, including their legal status, e.g., that marriage carries legal rights and protections not available to couples who are cohabiting or who have married, for example, in an unregistered religious ceremony.	
	Why marriage is an important relationship choice for many couples and why it must be freely entered into.	
	The characteristics and legal status of other types of long-term relationships.	
	The roles and responsibilities of parents with respect to the raising of children, including characteristics of successful parenting.	
	How to: determine whether other children, adults or sources of information are trustworthy; judge when a family, friend, intimate or other relationship is unsafe (and to recognise this in others' relationships); and how to seek help or advice, including reporting concerns about others, if needed.	
Respectful relationships including friendships	The characteristics of positive and healthy friendships (both on and offline) including: trust, respect, honesty, kindness, generosity, boundaries, privacy, consent and the management of conflict, reconciliation and ending relationships. This includes different (non-sexual) types of relationship.	
	Practical steps they can take in a range of different contexts to improve or support respectful relationships.	

	How stereotypes, in particular stereotypes based on sex, gender, race, religion, sexual orientation or disability, can cause damage (e.g., how they might normalise non-consensual behaviour or encourage prejudice).	
	That in school and in wider society they can expect to be treated with respect by others, and that in turn they should show due tolerance and respect to others and others' beliefs, including people in positions of authority and due tolerance of other peoples' beliefs.	
	About different types of bullying (including cyberbullying), the impact of bullying, responsibilities of bystanders to report bullying and how and where to get help.	
	That some types of behaviour within relationships are criminal, including violent behaviour and coercive control.	
	What constitutes sexual harassment and sexual violence and why these are always unacceptable.	
	The legal rights and responsibilities regarding equality (particularly with reference to the protected characteristics as defined in the Equality Act, 2010) and that everyone is unique and equal.	
Online and media	Their rights, responsibilities and opportunities online, including that the same expectations of behaviour apply in all contexts including online.	
	About online risks, including that any material someone provides to another has the potential to be shared online and the difficulty of removing potentially compromising material placed online.	
	Not to provide material to others that they would not want shared further and not to share personal material which is sent to them.	
	What to do and where to get support to report material or manage issues online.	
	The impact of viewing harmful content.	
	That specifically sexually explicit material, e.g., pornography often presents a distorted picture of sexual behaviours, can damage the way people see themselves in relation to others and negatively affect how they behave towards sexual partners.	

	That sharing and viewing indecent images of children (including those created by children) is a criminal offence which carries severe penalties including jail.	
	How information and data is generated, collected, shared and used online.	
Being safe	The concepts of, and laws relating to, sexual consent, sexual exploitation, abuse, grooming, coercion, harassment, rape, domestic abuse, forced marriage, honour-based violence and female genital mutilation (FGM), and how these can affect current and future relationships.	
	How people can actively communicate and recognise consent from others, including sexual consent, and how and when consent can be withdrawn (in all contexts including online).	
	How to recognise the characteristics and positive aspects of healthy one-to-one intimate relationships, which include mutual respect, consent, loyalty, trust, shared interests and outlook, sex and friendship.	
	That all aspects of health can be affected by choices they make in sex and relationships, positively or negatively, e.g., physical, emotional, mental, sexual and reproductive health and wellbeing.	
	The facts about reproductive health, including fertility and the potential impact of lifestyle on fertility for men and women.	
	That there are a range of strategies for identifying and managing sexual pressure, including understanding peer pressure, resisting pressure and not pressurising others.	
	That they have a choice to delay sex or to enjoy intimacy without sex.	
	The facts about the full range of contraceptive choices, efficacy and options available.	
	The facts around pregnancy, including miscarriage.	
	That there are choices in relation to pregnancy (with medically and legally accurate, impartial information on all options, including keeping the baby, adoption, abortion and where to get further help).	

	How the different sexually transmitted infections (STIs), including HIV/AIDS, are transmitted, how risk can be reduced through safer sex (including through condom use) and the importance of and facts about testing.	
	About the prevalence of some STIs, the impact they can have on those who contract them and key facts about treatment.	
	How the use of alcohol and drugs can lead to risky sexual behaviour.	
	How to get further advice, including how and where to access confidential sexual and reproductive health advice and treatment.	

2 Empowering Students to be Sexually Healthy

The Case for Teaching Sexual Health

It is common for schools to focus the majority of their RSE on sexual health, and in particular, risk management. Helping students to navigate risks around sex is, of course, important but this is not all there is to sexual health.

According to the World Health Organization (2006), sexual health is "...a state of physical, emotional, mental and social wellbeing in relation to sexuality; it is not merely the absence of disease, dysfunction or infirmity. Sexual health requires a positive and respectful approach to sexuality and sexual relationships, as well as the possibility of having pleasurable and safe sexual experiences, free of coercion, discrimination and violence. For sexual health to be attained and maintained, the sexual rights of all persons must be respected, protected and fulfilled."

As students develop their own agency regarding sex and relationships, they will acquire a greater sense of responsibility for their own sexual health. Additionally, if risks are taught against a backdrop of wellbeing in relation to sex, young people will be better equipped to adopt an empowered and positive approach to their sexual health and thus improve their sexual health outcomes (see the good sex / bad sex teaching activity from Chapter 1). Therefore, this chapter will be understood and implemented most effectively by first taking into account Chapter 1: Aims and Ethos.

A NOTE ON... Showing Photos of Diseased Genitals in RSE

Many schools show photos of diseased genitals in RSE, presumably to scare students into taking STIs seriously. However, as with all approaches to RSE, an evidenced approach is essential.

DOI: 10.4324/9781003437932-3

By showing the worst-case and often rare symptoms, young people may become less attuned to symptoms in their own bodies and miss STIs which are asymptomatic.

Showing worst-case examples like genitals marked by pus or warts may give the impression that teachers are exaggerating or distorting the truth and leave students feeling sexually demonised (Wilson et al., 2012). Indeed, the use of fear tactics in sex education can increase the learners' chances of adopting riskier behaviours (Hanson, 2022, cited in Sex Ed Forum, 2022; Lederer, 2016; McWhirter, 2008).

There is no place for fear tactics in RSE. When we teach risks, we must do so in a way that is evidence based and empowering. Providing students with scientific, medically accurate information, without engendering fear, is the most effective means of helping them to make healthy decisions (Wilson et al., 2012).

The evidence to support the efficacy of RSE in improving sexual health outcomes and reducing riskier sex is unequivocal. Combining a range of academic studies and their own research, the Sex Ed Forum's *Relationships and Sex Education: The Evidence* (2022) has demonstrated that good quality RSE has a tangible impact on young people's attitudes and behaviours in the following areas:

- Prevention of unintended pregnancies and STIs.
- Use of contraception when engaging in first-time sex and sex thereafter.
- Reduced riskier sexual behaviour.
- Delayed first-time sex.

Contrary to some of the moral hysteria around RSE, the evidence is clear: RSE does not sexualise young people. It does not lead them to having sex earlier, having more sex or having riskier sex. Rather, it equips them with the knowledge and skills to make empowered, informed and safer decisions.

TROUBLESHOOTING - Concerns from parents

This was discussed in more detail in Chapter 1. The evidence above can be used as part of your response to parents who raise concerns. Often, they will have seen headlines / social media posts, or statements from politicians which argue that RSE is sexualising and damaging young people. The evidence simply does not support this rhetoric. Show them the studies. Talk them through the evidence and make the case.

Local Services

Public Health investment and strategy to reduce instances of STIs and unwanted pregnancies in young people has been extensive. However, whilst the services exist, and most schools feel they are signposting them, young people often report that they are unaware of their rights to sexual health services or how to access these.

Therefore, in addition to a rigorous RSE programme, schools can empower students to be sexually healthy by bridging the gap between young people and sexual health services.

Top Tips

Effective signposting:

Consideration should be given to:

- When this is signposted to students (through RSE, assemblies, tutor time – repeat the information regularly).

- How a student would most easily find this information inside school (go-to members of staff, medical centre, pastoral leaders, posters in multiple locations, factsheets in the PSHE books).

- How a student would most easily find this information (and potentially in a state of panic) outside of school hours. (A one-stop-shop on the school website which is easily found and links to local services. Highlight how to find this when signposting services.)

- Student perception – even after delivering this information several times, check with students that they know where to access this information.

Information on accessing local sexual health services should include:

- A link to the local services website.

- Young people's right to access confidential contraception services at any age.

- Which local providers offer free condoms, hormonal contraceptives and emergency contraception (including pharmacies) and how to ask for this (it's not always offered) and how to access without a prescription.

- Bus routes to local services.

- Opening times for clinics, if they offer a walk-in service and if they need to book.

- What happens during an appointment – a walk though of questions that will be asked and how to respond.

- Online services: e.g., delivery of free condoms or chlamydia tests.

- Evening and weekend services.

- Access to abortion services.

RSE lessons can be used to increase understanding of:

- The risks of unprotected sex acts, including unwanted pregnancies and STIs.

- Understanding the pros and cons of different methods of contraception.

- Understanding how contraception is relevant from the perspective of their own gender and sexuality.

- Understanding the importance of STI testing and how this works, including home kits.

- Understanding the timeframe for emergency contraception.

- How to use condoms effectively.

- Abortion rights and options.

- What you offer as a school and how to access this (e.g., condoms, support, confidentiality, etc.).

CASE STUDY

With funding from Public Health, one local authority created a city-wide campaign to help young people to access local sexual health services. The steps they took included:

- Gathering a working group of young people to review the existing website and promotional materials.

- As a result of this, a one-stop-shop website was produced with input from young people. This was accompanied by a social media and poster campaign to be used by schools.

- A commitment was made from the local authority to fund ongoing work in this area to ensure that the information is kept up to date.

- The introduction of a pilot scheme where pharmacies in the city offer free, confidential contraception without prescription.

- A network of Secondary PSHE leads in the city was created.

- An RSE expert was commissioned to deliver training and provide teaching resources.

- Each PSHE lead reviewed the school's processes around signposting local services and fed back to the group.

- A central pledge was created including:

  ○ A commitment to signpost local services and the new website (multiple times to each year group in a variety of ways).

  ○ Explicit RSE lessons on contraception, confidentiality and local services.

  ○ Addition of a clear link to this on the school's website/ intranet (and for this to be highlighted to students every time local services are signposted).

  ○ A commitment to train all staff in this area.

  ○ Explicit go-to staff, including the school nurse and pastoral leaders.

  ○ Support offered to young people to access local services, including ringing ahead on their behalf, help with transport and additional help for those with special educational needs and disabilities (SEND).

A NOTE ON... Gillick Competency and Fraser Guidelines

Gillick Competency and Fraser Guidelines are often quoted when trying to balance the need to respect young people's agency with keeping them safe. Whilst distinct in their application, Gillick Competency and Fraser Guidelines both have their roots in the same court case from the 1980s which examined whether doctors should give contraception to under 16s without parental consent.

Gillick competence is used to assess whether a child has the capacity to make decisions for themselves and may be used to justify access to services without parents' consent (for example, confidential counselling or support for drug addiction). There are specific guidelines for medical professionals on how to make such an assessment.

The Fraser Guidelines are more specifically used to help children to confidentially access contraception, abortion and other sexual health services.

If a young person wants to access contraception, they should be encouraged to discuss this with their parents and supported to do so, if that is their wish. If they are reluctant to do so, this should be explored, and the professional should be vigilant for signs of abuse. Sexual activity involving a child under the age of 13 should always result in a Child Protection Referral (NSPCC, 2022)

Lifelong Sexual Health

When delivered effectively, RSE has the power to enhance students' sexual health whilst they are at school and for the rest of their lives.

STIs and unwanted pregnancy are a great place to start, but there are many more topics related to sexual health and health more broadly, which can promote an empowered attitude for life.

Other topics to consider include:

- The HPV vaccine: This is an early sexual health intervention. Empower students to see their own agency in this and to reflect upon the benefits of this early intervention.

- Taking responsibility for detecting cancer: Checking testicles and breasts for lumps and going for smear tests are important ways of protecting our health. Discuss these with students, give them space to express their concerns and help them to find ways to overcome these. There are some useful videos online which explore these issues.

- Fertility, pregnancy and birth: Help students to reflect on the options ahead for their future selves. Discuss ways in which these huge life events can be exciting and challenging. Reflect on what might be in their power to effect and what might not. Encourage students to think about how they might care for themselves if issues arise and how they might care for a partner.

- Menopause: There is increasing recognition that the widespread lack of understanding around menopause is something that needs to be corrected. Whether this affects their future selves, partners, colleagues or current family members, all students will benefit from increased knowledge and understanding of this issue. This can be explored in broader conversations about periods, puberty and body changes or listening to your body's needs or taught as a stand-alone topic.

- Sexual dysfunction: The NATSAL 3 survey found that one in six people in the UK had experienced a health condition that affected their sex life in the last year, yet fewer than one in four of these men and one in five of these women had sought help from a healthcare professional (NATSAL, 2010 in Mitchell et al., 2013). Discuss this with students. Part of an empowered approach towards sex involves recognising problems and seeking help if they arise. Whether this is anxiety about sex, porn addiction, vaginismus, erectile dysfunction, or anything else, help them to understand potential issues and how to address them.

TEACHER TOOLKIT

The Condom Demonstration Lesson

- Set the tone: Multiple studies have demonstrated that highlighting the benefits of using condoms rather than just focusing on the risks of not using them is most effective in improving students' sexual health outcomes in both the short and long term (Rigby et al., 1989). Therefore, a good starting point is to review your resources and the language you use in these lessons.

- Starter activity: Display a photo of a condom and ask groups to discuss all the potential benefits of condom use. Have a class discussion and highlight the many brilliant things about them, e.g.:

  - They are highly effective in preventing unwanted pregnancies.

  - They are highly effective in preventing STIs for both people and work for heterosexual people and men who have sex with men.

  - Unlike hormonal contraceptives, condoms help protect against both unwanted pregnancies and STIs.

  - They are easy to use (as we'll see later in the lesson).

  - They can add extra fun and pleasure (for both people) – some are flavoured and textured.

○ For some people, they can make sex last longer as the oversensitivity which leads to premature ejaculation is eased.

○ They can help both people feel more relaxed as they know, without question, that contraception is being used and they can focus on enjoying the moment.

○ It is usually quite obvious if the condom has broken. Therefore, emergency contraception and/or STI tests can be accessed quickly.

○ They provide a great opportunity to discuss consent. In a sexual moment you pause, discuss contraception and check you're both happy.

○ They can be used for multiple sex acts – vaginal, anal, oral (on a penis).

○ They are free! Highlight local services.

○ You can access them at an age and confidentially (remind them of their rights).

○ You can buy them everywhere – supermarkets, pharmacies, pub toilets.

○ Condom use reduces rates of cervical cancer.

○ Vegan and eco-friendly brands are available.

• The demo:

○ This should be fun! Whilst the subject matter is serious, the classroom atmosphere doesn't need to be. When students see you model comfort and ease, they will feel safer in engaging in the practical element of the lesson.

○ Have enough condom demonstrators so that there's one for the teacher and one between around four students. Ideally, the demonstrators should be blue or another non-racial colour. Some have suction pads on the bottom and you may want to stick your demonstrator to the board so students can get a better view. Issue every student with two condoms – one for the practical in the lesson and one to take home (ensure this has been agreed with senior leaders and is in your published RSE policy).

○ Ask the students to gather around and explain that condoms are approximately 98% effective if – and only if – they are used properly. If any of the following steps are missed out, that percentage begins to fall. As you explain the following points, physically demonstrate what you are doing with a condom and demonstrator:

- Check the condom is in date. Ask students to do this and ask what the date is on theirs. Ask what they should do if they find a condom is not in date (throw it away as the 98% may begin to decrease).

- Check the condom packet is intact. Do this together. Get them to feel the trapped air inside. Ask them what they should do if the package is perforated or screwed up (throw it away as the 98% will begin to decrease).

- Show them the jagged edge along the side and explain that this is where the condom package should be ripped. Explain that this needs to be done carefully so that the condom is not damaged. They should avoid using their teeth or scissors (if they do, that 98% may start to go down). Tell them not to open theirs yet.

- Ask them to watch you opening yours. Show them the condom and explain that one way of rolling it open will make it inside out and the other will be correct. It should roll outwards, away from the condom. Explain that it is essential that condoms are put on erect, rather than flaccid penises. However, in real life, after going through the stages above, the erection may have disap-peared. Reassure them that things like this happen. They may need to go back to some foreplay. When the penis is erect, as the demonstrator is, the condom can be put on. Explain that the teat of the condom needs to be squeezed with the fingers of one hand (this will prevent the condom from overstretching, which would reduce the 98%). Demonstrate this whilst using your other hand to unroll the condom down the shaft of the demon-strator. Explain that usually, as the sexual pleasure increases, the condom wearer will reach the point of orgasm and will ejaculate into the condom.

- Next, demonstrate how to remove the condom safely (if this is not done properly, the 98% will reduce). Explain that the penis will start to soften and shrink and the condom will become looser and could slip off. Show them how the condom can be secured at the top of the penis before being withdrawn and how, once away from their partner's body, it can be carefully removed without rolling it inside out or pinging it off. Show how the condom can be tied to secure the ejaculate, then wrapped in tissue, put in a bin and hands washed.

- Now let the students have a go. Move around the room as they do so. Spot any mistakes and give replacement condoms if necessary so the process can be repeated correctly.

TROUBLESHOOTING - Faith Schools

In schools where the teaching of contraception is viewed as contrary to the faith, signposting local services and reliable sources of information is even more crucial. Important subject matter should not be excluded, regardless of the school's perspective.

The statutory guidance states:

"All schools may teach about faith perspectives. In particular, schools with a religious character may teach the distinctive faith perspective on relationships, and balanced debate may take place about issues that are seen as contentious. For example, the school may wish to reflect on faith teachings about certain topics as well as how their faith institutions may support people in matters of relationships and sex."

(Department for Education, 2020).

It is possible and legitimate for faith schools to teach a range of perspectives, including their own. Therefore, a lesson on contraception or family planning can be structured around the view that children are a gift from God without omitting information on contraception, for example. Students might be asked to discuss why children are viewed as a gift and the ideal scenario in which this might come about. They might then reflect on why, even in a loving marriage, some believers choose to follow the rhythm method. This could be explored against different perspectives and methods like abstinence, contraception, abortion and so on with the faith perspective running throughout.

3   An Inclusive Approach to RSE

Diversity is a fact, but inclusion is a choice.

Common types of diversity include:

- Gender.

- Race and culture.

- LGBTQ+.

- Belief.

- Disability (body and neuro-diversity).

- Social mobility.

Inclusion means valuing difference and removing barriers to participation. It refers to the involvement and empowerment of a diverse range of individuals. Ensuring that our curriculum and approach is inclusive will ensure the empowerment of a diverse range of individuals whose uniqueness and integrity is respected and celebrated.

We all have a unique perspective and lens through which we view the world, and RSE will only be effective if students see themselves represented and understand how the content is relevant to them.

The statutory guidance states:

> "Pupils should be taught the facts and the law about sex, sexuality, sexual health and gender identity in an age-appropriate and inclusive way. All pupils should feel that the content is relevant to them and their developing sexuality. Sexual orientation and gender identity should be explored at a timely

DOI: 10.4324/9781003437932-4

point and in a clear, sensitive and respectful manner. When teaching about these topics, it must be recognised that young people may be discovering or understanding their sexual orientation or gender identity. There should be an equal opportunity to explore the features of stable and healthy same sex relationships. This should be integrated appropriately into the RSE programme, rather than addressed separately or in only one lesson."

(Department for Education, 2020).

In planning and delivering RSE content, it is important to consider the range of different perspectives we are likely to encounter. Chapter 1 discussed the importance of student consultation through both discursive working groups and anonymous surveys. The data generated from this will give your staff a greater sense of the diversity of perspectives within the student body and this can help to avoid making assumptions about students or using generalisations.

In any secondary classroom:

- Some may have watched hardcore porn, whilst others would be shocked by this.

- Some may be sexually experienced and others not.

- Some will be very interested in sex, and others repulsed by the idea.

- Some may believe that sex should only happen in marriage, whilst others will be hoping to get as much sexual experience as possible.

- Some may have high self-esteem, but others will not.

- Some will have parents that have regularly discussed sex with them, whilst other parents will never have broached the subject.

They will have different values, faiths, abilities, bodies, genders and sexualities, and our approach and language needs to bring everyone into the conversation.

TROUBLESHOOTING - Managing Different Perspectives

Some topics within RSE can become contentious and student discussions on these difficult to manage. For example, debates between students could emerge on: LGBTQ rights, abortion rights, promiscuity, porn and so on.

Creating a safe space for differences of opinion to be explored can be achieved by:

- Allowing discussion and differences of opinion.

- Reminding students of the school's aims and ethos, e.g., kindness, being a community, etc.

- Reminding students of the aims and ethos of empowering RSE - that each of them can decide for themselves (but not for others) what they think.

- Discuss wider debates that are happening on this issue and how it is inevitable that there will be difference of opinion in the room.

- Use opinion continuums (see the Teacher Toolkit) to train students how to challenge each other productively and respectfully.

- Use the Diversity Wheel task below to help students to reflect on the lens through which they view the world. This is also an opportunity to think about privilege, intersectionality and how we interact with others.

TEACHER TOOLKIT

Reflecting on the Lens through Which We View the World: The Diversity Wheel

This can be done at the start of an RSE topic and repeated again at the end as a way of helping students to link their learning to their own values and principles. It can also be a useful way to manage differences of opinion and belief.

Task

Look at the Diversity Wheel

- Choose five areas from the wheel (that you are happy to share) and share your profile with the person next to you, e.g., Muslim, student, British, etc.

- Discuss: In what ways do these aspects of your identity affect the way you view the world? In what ways might your diversity profile affect your views on sex and relationships?

- Which aspects of your diversity profile are most important to your sense of identity?

- Do you think any aspects of your profile might change in future? Are there others you think will be fixed for life?

- Which aspects of your identity put you in a majority group or minority group? With or without privilege? How might this affect the way that our opinions are formed? How might this affect how we experience the world?

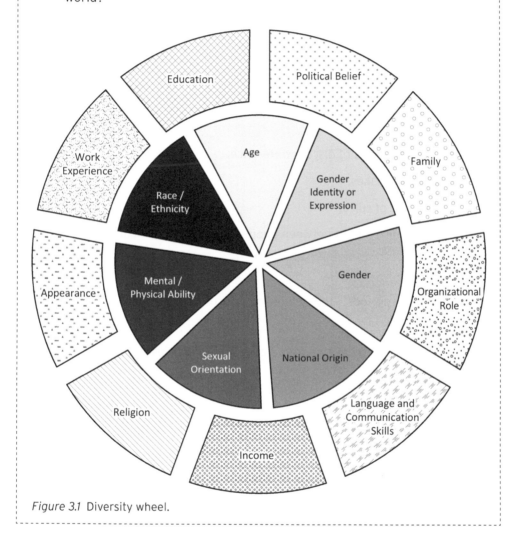

Figure 3.1 Diversity wheel.

A NOTE ON... Inclusive Language

Using inclusive language throughout RSE lessons is a way of making the content relevant to everyone.

Inclusive language...

is:

- An attempt to include and respect everyone.
- An ongoing learning process.
- Developed through conversation.
- An acknowledgement that words matter.

is not:

- Being too scared to discuss difference.
- Without mistakes.
- A fixed set of rules.
- Ignoring differences between people (e.g., 'I don't see colour').

Example:

In discussing periods, the following words/phrases may all be used interchangeably:

Women / people who have periods / people with ovaries / girls / trans boys / female-bodied people.

By using multiple terms, everyone is included.

CASE STUDY - Inclusive Case Studies in RSE

School X has undertaken an Equity, Diversity, and Inclusion (EDI) review of their RSE curriculum. Knowing that RSE has historically focused on male sexual pleasure and heterosexual sex and relationships, they have sought to identify and remedy where there are opportunities to embed a commitment to EDI in the curriculum and ensure that no student feels excluded.

When teaching sexual consent, for example, they use clips from popular TV shows to explore realistic, positive depictions of sexual consent and ensure that diversity is reflected in these.

Clip 1 (heterosexual couple): BBC series *Normal People* (also a book by Sally Rooney). Episode 2: 2.40–6.38.

In this scene, Connell (sexually experienced) and Marianne (no sexual experience) have sex for the first time. They openly ask each other what feels good, if this is what they want and if they have condoms (they do). Students are asked to observe then discuss all the ways that consent is asked for and given in verbal and non-verbal ways. How do they show that it's a 'hell yes' for both of them?

WARNING – Features nudity and sexual content – please give opt-out.

Clip 2 (heterosexual couple, one of them disabled): Netflix series *Sex Education*. Season 3 Episode 4, when a dinner date between Isaac and Maeve becomes intimate. Isaac is paralysed from the chest down. Maeve starts kissing him, then pulls away. "Can …" she whispers, trailing off.

"You want to know what I can feel?" Isaac asks. "Yeah," Maeve replies. "Well, I can't feel anything below my level of injury," Isaac says. "If you put your hand on my chest, I'll show you." Students are invited to discuss how consent was navigated and how Maeve showed her sensitivity towards his disability.

Clip 3 (same-sex female, mixed-race couple): Netflix series *Heartstopper*. Season 1, Episode 3, which features many scenes of same-sex couples navigating consent in an authentic and positive way. At a party, Darcy and Tara kiss on the dance floor. Students are encouraged to discuss the non-verbal ways in which they both show that they are consenting to the kiss.

TEACHER TOOLKIT

Inclusion of Different Faith Perspectives

Example: Family Planning

A lesson on family planning is a good opportunity to explore different faith perspectives and to allow students to develop their own views and ability to think critically.

- Set the scene:
  - Many heterosexual couples spend a lot of their lives trying to avoid pregnancy.
  - During this time, an accidental pregnancy can be a difficult thing to deal with.

- Discussion:
  - What options are available in this situation?
  - Explore different options (you might want to use case studies):
    - Keep the baby.
    - Adoption.
    - Take emergency contraception (up to five days after sex).
    - Terminate the pregnancy – abortion.
  - Ask students to discuss the pros and cons of the above.
  - Explore differences of opinion in a non-judgemental way, for example, by discussing divergent views on the ethics of abortion.
  - Explore the UK law on abortion and local services and ask students to reflect on their own views in relation to questions like:
    - What would happen if abortion was made illegal?
    - What should come first – the rights of the mother or the rights of the foetus?
    - Should late-term abortions be banned or is it necessary for these to be allowed? Has UK law got this right?
    - Teenagers are the group most likely to experience unwanted pregnancies. What should be done about this?
    - Do you agree that prospective fathers should not have a legal say in abortions?
    - How can men empower themselves when it comes to family planning?

TROUBLESHOOTING

Differing perspectives on topics like abortion can be difficult to manage and it is important that the teacher delivering this feels confident and empowered to do so.

Concern about upsetting students:

Before beginning every RSE topic, run through the topics that will be covered. Explain to students that they can privately contact you before teaching begins if they have any concerns. This trigger warning should help to avoid a situation where a student feels particularly uncomfortable or upset. If a student does come to see you, this may be indicative of a safeguarding issue and vigilance regarding this is important.

Teacher discomfort:

- As with all RSE topics, as a teacher, you are not revealing anything about your own experiences or beliefs. Remind students of this and adopt a non-judgemental approach.

- Before you begin an open discussion tell students to expect a range of views on this issue and to be respectful and sensitive to this. Encourage diversity of thought and critical thinking.

- Remind students how they can respectfully challenge each other. For example, "I understand your point but have you considered…"

- You might like to use an opinion continuum where, rather than asking open questions, you read statements and ask students to physically place themselves along a wall, according to how strongly they agree or disagree. You might want to ask volunteers to justify their position. As always, allow an opt-out.

- If you still feel uncomfortable, it might be worth team teaching with a colleague who is more at ease with this topic.

A NOTE ON... SEND and RSE

There is no singular approach to planning and delivering RSE for students with acute SEND. The specific needs of each individual student may necessitate a targeted approach to ensure that barriers to their participation are removed. For students with the most significant needs, their Educational Health Care (EHC) assessment should be used to create a tailored approach for their EHC plan.

The Sex Ed Forum's 'RSE for disabled pupils and pupils with Special Educational Needs' (2020) is an excellent guide to help begin your planning.

LGBTQ+ Inclusion in RSE

LGBTQ+ inclusion is not a 'one and done'; rather, it should be embedded throughout all aspects of RSE.

In addition to this, LGBTQ+ inclusion as subject matter is also an important part of the curriculum and helps students to reflect on their own identities and questions about human existence.

TEACHER TOOLKIT

LGBTQ+ as Subject Matter: A Lesson on Sex/Gender/Sexuality

Issue students with A2 paper and board pens.

Group Task

- On large paper write the terms *sex*, *gender* and *sexuality*.
- Discuss and record your ideas on:
    - How do we know the sex/gender/sexuality of an individual?
    - What labels are associated with each category?

Allow 15 minutes for the group task and 15 minutes for class feedback and discussion.

Explain to students:

Whilst there is much debate about these concepts, there is often agreement that…

Sex is a biological feature and known through chromosomes, hormones and genitals.

Categories: male, female, intersex.

Gender identity is often regarded as a psychological feature, part of our internal identity and the way we view ourselves.

Gender expression is what we show to the world and based on social norms, e.g., what we wear and the pronouns we use. These are often associated with masculinity or femininity.

Labels include:

Cis gender: sex and gender are congruent.

Transgender: sex and gender are incongruent.

Non-binary: do not identify with either end of the gender binary.

Sexuality refers to sexual and romantic attraction.

Labels include: gay, straight, bisexual, pansexual, asexual, queer.

Pansexual: people who do not acknowledge the gender binary in their sexual attraction. They are attracted to an individual because of who they are, rather than the box they fit into.

Asexual: not sexually attracted to anyone.

Personal reflections/discussion questions:

Is sex/gender/sexuality binary?

Are these aspects of ourselves fixed or fluid?

Does it matter?

A NOTE ON… Understanding Different Identities

A note on intersex: Approximately 1.7% of the population is intersex (Amnesty International, 2018). In most cases, human conception follows one of two routes, dictated by whether the successful sperm is a X or Y chromosome. The X chromosome generates a female foetus (which produces oestrogen and female genitals), and the Y chromosome generates a male foetus (which produces testosterone and male genitals). In 1.7% of cases this does not happen as expected, leading to a range of conditions which fit under the intersex umbrella. Sometimes this is evident at birth, as the genitals are indeterminate. In other cases, this becomes apparent during puberty or later, if reproductive problems are experienced.

Even in nature, there is no such thing as a total binary. Use this as an interesting discussion point.

A note on queer: Whilst this was once a pejorative term, some LGBTQ+ people have chosen to reclaim and embrace queer as a positive. Queer Theory is a post-modern academic approach which seeks to destabilise and subvert categories which designate some identities as normative, e.g., heterosexual, and others as deviant, e.g., homosexual. Many people today use the term 'queer' interchangeably with 'gay.' For others, queer is associated with a fluid understanding of gender and sexuality. Some LGBT people reject the term queer, regarding the label of lesbian, for example, as distinct and important.

A note on non-binary / gender fluid / gender queer: These terms are often used interchangeably but can be understood to have different meanings:

- Non-binary (NB) can be understood as existing outside of the binary categories of male and female. For some NB people, there can be an incongruence and discomfort with being associated with both male and female, masculine and feminine. This is different to intersex, which refers to a biological condition. Many NB people (although not all) prefer to be referred to with gender-neutral pronouns like 'they/them.' Some experience trauma when forced into gendered categories, e.g., in school sports or changing facilities.

- Gender fluid is a term sometimes used by people who have a fluid understanding and experience of their gender identity and expression. They may feel comfortable being referred to with the gendered pronouns that match their sex assigned at birth but also use gender-neutral pronouns.

- Gender Queer is often used in a similar way. For some, gender expression is regarded as a performance and they may adopt a playful approach towards this, for example, performing butch gender on one day and fem on another.

A note on asexual: Some students will identify as asexual. For most, this means that they do not experience sexual desire. RSE lessons can be difficult for these students if the teacher's language and approach convey the assumption that all students will feel sexual desire. It is important to help all students understand what asexual means, to legitimise this as one, valid identity amongst many others and to help these students to feel reassured and empowered to set their own boundaries.

A note on gender-critical (GC) feminism: GCs may reject the above separation of sex and gender and regard them as immutable. They usually reject the term 'cis.' They often regard the advancement of trans rights as a threat to women's rights and some state that sex (including gender) cannot change. GCs are sometimes referred to as TERFs (Trans Exclusive Radical Feminists). Whilst some GCs regard TERF as a slur, others have embraced the term.

A note on trans rights:

- Interpretation of the Equality Act, 2010

  - The lack of national, legally assured guidance means that schools are currently attempting to interpret the Equality Act. Since much of this is yet to be tested in the courts, different schools are adopting different approaches.

  - The government's repeated delays in publishing the long-awaited trans guidance for schools is evidence of what a socially and legally contentious issue this has become.

  - The Equality Act, 2010 includes 'Gender reassignment' as one of the nine protected characteristics:

    - "A person has the protected characteristic of gender reassignment if the person is proposing to undergo, is undergoing or has undergone a process (or part of a process) for the purpose of reassigning the person's sex by changing physiological or other attributes of sex." (Equality Act, 2010).

- The DfE later said "… in order to be protected under the Act, a pupil will not necessarily have to be undertaking a medical procedure to change their sex but must be taking steps to live in the opposite gender or proposing to do so." (Department for Education, 2014).

- And: "It is relatively rare for pupils – particularly very young pupils – to want to undergo gender reassignment, but when a pupil does so a number of issues will arise which will need to be sensitively handled. There is evidence that the number of such cases is increasing and schools should aim to address any issues early on and in a proactive way." (Department for Education, 2014).

  - Some regard single-sex (cis only) spaces as protected by the Act. Others regard gender-critical beliefs as a philosophical belief protected by the Act (BBC News, 2021).

  - Some have argued that this protection does not apply to children. This view was publicly stated in 2022 by the then Attorney General, Suella Braverman, who claimed that under-18s cannot legally change their gender and that schools should not 'pander' to trans children (Swinford, 2022).

  - 78% of teachers want more support to help trans students (Just Like Us, 2022).

  - Two thirds of the general public support trans issues being taught in schools (More in Common, 2022).

- The broader picture:

  - Many young trans people receive inadequate support and are more likely to be bullied, suffer mental health problems, self-harm and attempt suicide (Stonewall, 2017).

  - There was a 56% rise in hate crimes against trans people in 2021–22 (BBC News, 2022).

  - Politically, trans rights have become a contentious issue. Some have accused the current government of using trans issues to stoke the 'culture wars.' The Prime Minister joking about trans people, (Walker, 2023) and the exclusion of trans people from the ban on conversion therapy (Hinsliff, 2022) have been cited as evidence of this.

- ○ On social media, the debate over trans rights has become polarised and vicious. Some activists on both sides have used these platforms to publicly and personally attack their opponents. Elon Musk, the owner of X (previously Twitter) has declared that the terms 'cis' and 'cisgender' will be regarded as slurs on the platform (Elsesser, 2023).

- ○ Ipso recorded a 400% increase in press coverage of trans people from 2014–2019 (Julian, 2020).

- ○ According to the 2021 Census of England and Wales, trans people make up just 0.6% of the population (Office for National Statistics, 2023).

- Tips for schools:

  - ○ Training and education – staff and students: Carefully research external speakers who can provide empowering, positive training which provides space for questioning and positive curiosity.

  - ○ Monitor: At the time of writing, the schools' trans guidance has been delayed again. The picture is rapidly evolving. Carefully monitor what happens in the courts, leaked guidance, which new guidance is published and what is statutory.

  - ○ Take pre-emptive measures. For example, make all uniform and sports kit non-gendered e.g., 'skirt and trouser' uniform, rather than 'girl and boy', allow students to be referred to by nicknames in class to avoid trans and non-binary students having to 'out' themselves.

  - ○ Actively celebrate difference as a school through Pride Societies and so on. Embrace, rather than tolerate, difference.

  - ○ Ensure all RSE is fully inclusive.

TEACHER TOOLKIT

Embedding LGBTQ+ Inclusion in the RSE Curriculum

Example 1: Contraception

Approaches to sexual health, including the condom lesson were discussed in Chapter 2. As with all aspects of RSE, LGBTQ inclusion should be threaded throughout lessons on sexual health. Top tips:

- When introducing sexual health, ask students to identify who needs to engage with this. Answer:
  - Men who have sex with women.
  - Women who have sex with men.
  - Men who have sex with men.
  - Women who have sex with women.
  - Trans and non-binary people.
  - Intersex people.
  - Bisexual people.
  - EVERYONE who is sexually active.

- When talking about condoms, consistently avoid heteronormative assumptions. Make it clear that anyone with a penis who is sexually active will benefit from their use (unless they have been tested and are in a long-term relationship / would welcome a pregnancy, etc.).

- Differentiate between different types of sex act and the associated risks (oral, vaginal, anal). Include the use of non-gendered language, e.g., 'partner,' 'person with the penis,' 'person receiving the penis.' When exploring this with case studies, include examples with different genders and sexualities.

- Different sex acts have different levels of risk and it is important to be transparent about this. Ask students to rank body fluids exchanged during sex acts according to the risk of STIs:

1. Blood.

2. Semen.

3. Vaginal fluid.

4. Saliva.

Then discuss which sex acts may be riskier than others and which groups of people may be at greater risk. For example, people of any gender or sexuality who have anal sex are engaging in a riskier sex act (blood and semen may be exchanged). Against this backdrop, discuss ways in which risks can be reduced, e.g., barrier contraception, water-based lubricant, access to sexual health services, regular testing, honesty, communication, etc. Give this information without judgement. Every student can view this through their own lens and work out which aspects of their learning are most pertinent to them personally.

Students will identify that one of the lower risk sex acts is oral sex on a female-bodied person (who may have a partner of any gender). However, it is important to note that this is not without risk. The HPV vaccine helps mitigate some of the risk, but many people choose to use dental dams (a layer of latex placed over the vulva) for additional protection. These are more expensive and difficult to source than condoms but can be bought in many pharmacies and online. Show these to students when you do the condom lesson.

Example 2: Family Planning

Make the relevance to all genders and sexualities explicit throughout.

When discussing routes to family planning, for example, highlight to whom this may be relevant:

- Natural conception (male and female bodies).

- Fertility treatments (heterosexual), e.g., IVF – In Vitro Fertilisation; AID – Artificial Insemination (Donor); AIH – Artificial Insemination (Husband/partner).

- Fertility treatments (two females), e.g., IVF/AID.

- Surrogacy (heterosexual and homosexual) – surrogate's egg or intended mother's egg.

- Adoption (all genders and sexualities).

When exploring infertility:

- Some people need assistance in conceiving a baby. This can be because:

  ○ The person is single.

  ○ It's a same-sex relationship.

  ○ One or both people in a heterosexual relationship experience fertility difficulties, e.g., low sperm count or eggs which are not viable.

These small tweaks to ensure that your teaching of sexual health is LGBTQ+ inclusive can be applied to all aspects of your RSE curriculum.

4   Understanding Bodies, Sex and Pleasure

RSE usually starts with bodies but the approach to this can be skewed and have little impact. It is a good idea to review the existing approach and ask the following:

- Is the approach phallocentric (only focused on the penis and male sexual pleasure)?

- If the approach is biological, has consideration been given to the relevance and usefulness of this material? For example, biological diagrams of the penis and uterus might be used when teaching reproduction, but are these diagrams useful when trying to understand other aspects of sex? Is there a diagram of the vulva? When discussing male ejaculation is female sexual pleasure also discussed? Is the clitoris featured? Female ejaculation and so on.

- Do the materials reinforce heteronormativity – i.e., an exclusive focus on heterosexual sex and reproduction?

- Are the materials inclusive? Are different races, genders and bodies represented?

- What are the aims and ethos? Is empowerment embedded? (See Chapter 1).

- Have you consulted students about how impactful they find these lessons? Are you embedding their feedback in your planning? (See Chapter 1).

Beyond Biology

Whilst it can feel safer to rely on biological approaches to RSE, this approach is limited. Relationships, power, pleasure, porn and so much more require a far broader and more nuanced approach. Even topics closely associated with biology like puberty and pregnancy will be more engaging and impactful if based on lived experience and life skills. The following examples show how a biological approach can be a starting point but will become so much more in RSE:

DOI: 10.4324/9781003437932-5

Biological starting point	Moving beyond this:
Periods: monthly cycle, links to reproduction, etc.	Periods: the joys and challenges of growing up, self-awareness of mood and body changes, empathy with others, accessing sanitary products, destigmatising periods, men who bleed, period poverty, etc.
Reproduction: natural and artificial means of reproduction, fertility, pregnancy, birth, etc.	Reproduction: an empowered approach to family planning, ethical considerations, local services, who to speak to, how to navigate difficult conversations, etc.
Sexual intercourse: male ejaculation, contraception, etc.	Sexual intercourse: what is sex? What is virginity and is this the same for everyone, how do you know when the time is right, what to expect, what can go wrong, consent, LGBTQ sex, pleasure, empowerment, etc.

Sexual Anatomy

Accurate anatomical terms for genitals are important for children of all ages; at home and at school. Using the correct terms for brain, knee, ear, etc. but not genitals can embed a sense of shame and secrecy around sex. Using euphemisms can make it more difficult for children to name problems with their genitals and to report abuse.

Accurate terms like 'vulva', 'penis', 'anus', etc. are not sexual words. When introduced to children early and used throughout their childhood, they become neutral and useful. The common misuse use of the word 'vagina' to refer to the vulva, for example, may seem like a harmless inaccuracy, but this is indicative of a widespread ignorance about the female genitalia. Empowering young people with body literacy helps them to understand changes as they occur, identify and communicate any issues, develop positive body image and, ultimately, to empower them when it comes to sex.

TEACHER TOOLKIT

Understanding Genitals

This is a fun lesson and not meant to be taken too seriously.

Issue students with Play-Doh for modelling or pen and paper for drawing. Explain that we are going to create models/drawings of genitals. Divide your whiteboard in half and write 'female' on one side and 'male' on the other. Ask

---

the class what each is called and what parts they are aware of for each. Record their ideas. This will probably expose a greater understanding of the male anatomy. Unpack this with them. Correct them if they use the word 'vagina' for the external female genitals. Explain that the vagina is inside the body and that the correct term is vulva. By the end of the discussion ensure you have the following:

Penis – shaft, glans, urethra, foreskin / no foreskin, scrotum, anus.

Vulva – clitoris, clitoral hood, labia minora, labia majora, urethra, vaginal opening, anus.

Ask them to model/draw each in turn and to include all features listed.

Ask them which was most difficult and why. Usually, they find the vulva far more difficult and some do not know where to begin.

Talk through accurate photos/drawings/models of each. Show lots of different examples of genitals and discuss the variation in size, colour and appearance. Discuss insecurities that some people experience regarding the appearance of their genitals. Explain that this can be a barrier to pleasure and help students to think about how positive body image might be a feature of good sex. People are more likely to enjoy sex if they are present in the moment rather than focused on insecurities about their appearance.

Gender Equity

We have all seen penises drawn on exercise books and lockers. We have all seen biological diagrams of penises (both erect and flaccid). We have all been presented with the notion that discussions of male sexual anatomy are a legitimate and essential part of any RSE course. Despite this, featuring the vulva, clitoris, female orgasm, female ejaculation etc. are still regarded by many as somehow different, taboo and over sexualised.

A phallocentric approach may be viewed as the default but in reality, this is a choice rooted in misogyny. We owe it to our students to correct this erasure and model gender equity in our teaching of RSE. In addition to the above task on understanding genitals, time should be spent unpacking female sexual pleasure as an important remedy to the pervasive ignorance and misinformation.

TEACHER TOOLKIT

Educating Students about Female Sexual Pleasure

- Share facts about the clitoris:

  ○ The clitoris has 8,000 nerve endings (double that of the penis). Across the vulva and vagina there are around 15,000 nerve endings.

  ○ The only function of the clitoris is sexual pleasure.

  ○ It's just the tip of the iceberg.

  ○ Most women do not orgasm from penetration alone.

  ○ Many women are capable of multiple orgasms.

  ○ Some women ejaculate.

  ○ Some women fake orgasms.

- Show a model or drawing of the 3D, internal clitoris. Show this in comparison to the vulva and explain that a clitoral orgasm can happen from external and internal stimulation. Women are more likely to orgasm from stimulation of the external clitoris.

- Discussion questions:

  ○ Is female sexual pleasure depicted in an accurate way in porn? What might the differences be? Pick up on:

    ▪ Porn is usually made by men for a male audience.

    ▪ Porn stars are paid more to do sexual acts which cause them discomfort/pain.

    ▪ Depictions of female pleasure are often fake and exaggerated.

    ▪ In real life, people may need to feel relaxed, safe and have an intimate connection to be able to orgasm.

  ○ Some women fake orgasms – why? Pick up on:

    ▪ There may be a lack of understanding from one or both partners about how this works.

    ▪ Her partner may be mimicking things from porn.

    ▪ For some women, the orgasm can be difficult to master with a partner or alone. They may not be ready or able in that moment.

- The women may feel obliged to make her partner feel that they've done a good job.

- Internalised misogyny may mean that the woman only values her partner's pleasure and not her own.

  ○ Is faking orgasms a good idea? Pick up on:

- How does this relate to good sex / bad sex? Communication, trust, etc.

- Her partner may think they have discovered what to do and keep doing the same thing.

- This may become a barrier to pleasure.

- The orgasm gap

  ○ Look at stats on the orgasm gap (Frederick et al., 2018):

  ○ 95% of heterosexual men always orgasm with a partner compared with 65% of heterosexual women.

  ○ What might explain this? Note that 86% of lesbian women always orgasm with a partner.

Understanding Sex and Virginity

Our understanding of sex and virginity is tied up in historical heteronormativity and patriarchy. Unpacking this is an important part of empowering young people to tune into what they really want.

TEACHER TOOLKIT

- Ask groups to come up with a definition for the act of sex.

- Ask groups to come up with a definition for virginity and what needs to happen for a person to lose their virginity.

- Take answers. Are there different views? Lead a discussion:

  ○ Are all answers heteronormative? Do all answers involve a penis? What about LGBTQ people? Unpack together.

  ○ Is there such a thing as virginity? Some people regard an intact hymen as being the mark of virginity. However, only women have

> hymens and approximately half of them will break their hymen before having penetrative sex, e.g., from cycling or using a tampon.
>
> ○ What are some of the historical/traditional meanings behind virginity?

Share and discuss some of the cultural norms and obligations around virginity:

- In Western culture, virginity is still seen as a valuable commodity by many, a special thing which should not be easily given away. 'Losing' your virginity can be seen as a loss of purity and, in some cases, desirability.

- Women are often 'slut shamed' and subjected to double standards for having sex when men are not judged in same way.

- Virginity is heteronormative and implies a specialness linked exclusively to penis in vagina penetration. This can diminish same-sex sex and give the impression that other kinds of sex are not important.

- Virginity is usually conceived as requiring the male ejaculation with no reference to female sexual pleasure.

- Historically, and still in some cultures, fathers pay a dowry to their daughter's new husband. The price and agreement are often dependent upon the bride's virginity being intact.

- Approximately 200 million women and girls have been subjected to female genital mutilation (World Health Organisation, 2023). One of the main reasons for this is to ensure chastity before marriage and thus guarantee the virginity of the bride.

- Women are murdered in so-called honour killings for losing their virginity before marriage, even when this is the result of rape.

- Virginity tests are conducted in many countries. This involves two fingers being inserted into the vagina, sometimes without consent. This is not an accurate measure and girls/women deemed to have had sex can be disregarded as impure.

- In some countries there are medical professionals who specialise in making a new bride appear to be a virgin when she is not.

Discussion: What does virginity mean today? Has this changed? Is it a useful concept?

First-Time Sex

First-time sex can be a big deal. There's a huge amount to consider: when, where, how, who, contraception, consent, performance and so on. RSE can help young people to approach this positively and to begin the rest of their sex lives with a sense of empowerment.

TEACHER TOOLKIT

Promoting Self-Awareness and Agency

Helping students to develop self-awareness around sex and relation-ships is a key component of an empowering approach. By emphasising their agency, we can encourage young people to ask the following of themselves:

- Why do I want to do this? Is this an empowered choice, based on my own desire or the result of other factors like social pressure, pressure from a partner, messages from porn, etc.?

- Is this the right time? Have we got contraception? Is this legal? Have we had too much alcohol to drink?

- How am I treating my partner? Am I sure that they really want this? Am I checking in with them? Is there a sense of mutual respect between us?

- Am I feeling it in the moment? Is this giving me pleasure? Do I feel I can stop if I want to? Are things going at the right pace?

- What emotions am I feeling most strongly?

Show students the questions above and ask them to discuss green/red flags. What might indicate they're going to be happy about this afterwards and what might indicate the opposite?

Ensuring first-time sex is a positive experience:

- Issue students with large paper and board pens.

- Brainstorm 1: Worries people might have about first-time sex.

  ○ Worries might include – pain, not being ready, making a mistake, con-traception, pregnancy, parents finding out, the other person not lik-ing them anymore, feeling under pressure etc.

- ○ What can be done? Ask them to add ideas in a different colour next to each worry.

- ○ Discuss and unpack, e.g., pain – possible solutions: being ready and relaxed, water-based lubricant, foreplay, etc.

- Brainstorm 2: Red flags / signs it might not be the right time.

  - ○ Discuss and unpack, e.g., if – you are very worried, you don't have contraception, you're drunk, you don't feel ready, you're doing it because you feel under pressure from the other person or your friends, you don't fancy the person, you are not physically ready etc.

- Brainstorm 3: Green flags / signs it might be the right time

  - ○ Discuss and unpack, e.g., if – you feel physically and emotionally ready, you trust or love the other person, you are feeling turned on, you think you will enjoy it, you are doing it because you want to, you're in the right place, you have contraception, you are sure the other person wants to do it, etc.

Ask groups to discuss the following case studies and give advice for each:

Leon (15)	Sara (15)
"All my mates have had sex. I've told them I've lost my virginity but I haven't really. I've got a girlfriend but she's a virgin too and says she isn't ready. What can I do?"	"My boyfriend (Leon) keeps pressuring me to have sex with him. I think I love him but I'm just not ready yet. I feel bad about saying no and he keeps going on at me. What can I do?"
Tariq (16)	**Sam (16)**
"I feel under so much pressure to lose my virginity. My boyfriend and I keep trying but every time we do I get nervous and lose my erection. What can I do?"	"I'm about to have sex for the first time. I don't have a condom. As she hasn't mentioned it, I'm guessing she's on the pill. I don't want to ruin the mood by asking. What can I do?"
Abs (15)	**Becky (14)**
"My girlfriend and I have been having sex for three months. Everyone in porn does anal but she won't do it. What can I do?"	"My girlfriend has been fingering me, but it really hurts. She seems to like it on her, but I find it really uncomfortable. I've been pretending I like it, but I really don't. I want to try something different. What can I do?"

Arousal:

- Ask students to discuss and record what sexual arousal might involve physically, emotionally and mentally. Discuss ideas.
  - Physically: swollen, wet, tingly genitals, feeling physically drawn to the other person, longing for more.
  - Emotionally: excited, nervous, lust, closeness.
  - Mentally: feeling present, knowing the time is right, checking in with yourself and your partner, "this is amazing!"
- Other things to note:
  - Arousal can come and go quickly.
  - It's possible to be mentally aroused but not physically and vice versa.
  - Lots of arousal can lead to premature ejaculation.
  - It is okay to stop, even if both people are aroused.
  - It is possible to be ready and still feel nervous.

Opinion Continuum

Ask students to stand at the back of the class. As each statement is read out, they should physically position themselves according to where their opinion fits. Ask volunteers to justify their response to each statement and allow for discussion.

1. Men are always ready for sex.
2. If a man has an erection, it means he wants sex.
3. It is obvious if your partner is ready for sex.
4. First-time sex will be painful.
5. Women are more likely to enjoy sex if they have had foreplay first.
6. Being emotionally ready for sex means you are ready.
7. If you love someone you will have sex with them.
8. It's okay to persuade your partner to have sex.
9. Contraception is the responsibility of both people.
10. Sex will feel better if both people are truly ready for it.

A NOTE ON... Anal Sex

With 'anal' being the 5th most popular category on Pornhub in 2022 (Pornhub, 2022), many young people see this as a standard and desirable sexual practice. In addition to discussing this in the context of lessons on sexual health (see Chapter 2) and Pornography (see Chapter 7), many students will be curious about the extent to which this is pleasurable. Refusing to engage with this leaves students vulnerable to misinformation and pressure to conform to norms from porn. Discussions on this should be factual and non-judgemental.

In a discussion on this with older students, the following points could be explored:

- Anal sex is very Marmite – some people love it, some people hate it (both giving and receiving).

- In Britain, the National Survey of Sexual Attitudes and Lifestyle showed an increase in participation in heterosexual anal sex in 16- to 24-year-olds from 12.5% to 28.5% over the last few decades (*British Medical Journal*, no date).

- Although anal sex is everywhere in porn, for most people, it is not a regular part of their sex lives (Erens et al., 2013).

- It is possible for people of any sex to achieve an orgasm from anal sex alone. However, anal sex is more likely to be pleasurable for men. Men have a prostate gland which is stimulated by anal sex and can be very pleasurable.

- Some people build up to anal sex over time by gently experimenting with smaller sex toys / fingers.

- Only specialist sex toys with a base should be used in the anus (other toys can become sucked into the body).

- Some people try anal sex and find it extremely painful so never do so again.

- Increasingly, doctors are treating people with problems caused by anal sex, particularly women for faecal incontinence and anal sphincter injury (*British Medical Journal*, no date).

- Although it is difficult to get pregnant from anal sex it is possible if the person receiving is female and a condom is not used. Semen can leak from the anus into the vagina.

- Consent is everything. Up to 25% of women with experience of anal sex report they have been pressured into it at least once (*British Medical Journal*, no date).

- The way anal sex is depicted in a lot of porn would be very painful in real life.

- Some people think all gay men have anal sex, but this is not the case. A 2018 survey by Bespoke Surgical found that 29% of gay men chose bottoming / receiving anal as their favourite position (Goldstein, 2018).

- Anal sex is a riskier sex act (see Chapter 2).

- Safer and more pleasurable anal sex may involve:

  ○ Condoms.

  ○ Water-based lubricant.

  ○ Careful communication.

  ○ Douching (cleaning out the anus with warm water).

5 Sexual Consent for All

In all likelihood, most of us teaching RSE received either inadequate teaching on sexual consent or none at all. In my own school, the only time this was addressed was when a visiting speaker (possibly the police) came in to give a talk. The boys were sent outside to play football (really!) whilst the girls were taught how to not get raped. We were given rape alarms and lectured about not being alone at night or putting ourselves in a vulnerable position. It was terrifying.

Happily, things have moved on. The teaching of consent forms part of the statutory framework, and most schools now address this with all students (not just girls). However, the lack of teacher training in this area, quality resources and rigorous impact assessments means that the provision is inconsistent and its impact unclear.

For some boys, the experience of these lessons can engender a sense of defensiveness. Some describe feeling scared of beginning their sex lives, worried that they will get this wrong or be accused of crossing the line when they haven't. Some girls still report the messaging of these lessons reinforcing victim blaming and shame around female sexuality with 'boys will be boys' tropes going unchallenged. For LGBTQ students, the lessons can fail to resonate when consent is only referred to within a heteronormative framework.

Sexual consent is the foundation of everything when it comes to sex, and making this case to students is essential. The approach, as with all aspects of RSE, should be one that goes beyond risk management, is evidence based and is empowering and relevant to all students.

DOI: 10.4324/9781003437932-6

A NOTE ON... **Sexual Pleasure**

Although many teachers find discussions on sexual pleasure difficult, incorporating this in your teaching of consent (and all other aspects of RSE) will make the lessons far more impactful. This is discussed, with suggested practical activities in Chapter 1 and Chapter 4.

Sexual consent only makes sense against a backdrop of sexual pleasure. When young people understand that sex should feel good and develop the skills to communicate with themselves and their partners about this, they are much more likely to get consent right.

Dated notions about male/female sexuality are still prevalent and combatting these will enhance our teaching of consent. For example, unpacking and challenging the following ideas can help with this:

- Men are sex crazed.
- Men are sexually dominant.
- Male sexual pleasure is the only goal.
- Female sexuality is shameful.
- Sex should hurt.
- We shouldn't hurt our partner's feelings.
- All women orgasm from penetration alone.

TEACHER TOOLKIT

Emphasising the Importance of Sexual Consent

Sexual consent is the foundation of everything when it comes to sex. Think back to the 'setting the tone' activity from Chapter 1 when students identified the features of good/bad sex. Refer back to their posters or the photo of your notes from the class discussion. Ask groups to discuss – how is consent relevant to each of the features of good/bad sex? For example:

- Good sex:
  - Contraception: Both people consent to sex with or without contraception. Transparent communication.

- ○ Orgasms: Much more likely to happen if both people are enjoying what is happening and psychologically relaxed and happy.

- ○ Trust: The foundation of consent. When consent is violated, this is a betrayal of trust.

- Bad sex:

  - ○ Painful: Respecting consent and checking in with each other will help to avoid this. Asking yourself: Is this what I want, does it feel good and communicating this. Checking in with your partner.

  - ○ Exploitation: Ensuring that both people consent will avoid this before, during and after the sex act. Fully informed and empowered consent for both people.

  - ○ Regret afterwards: Setting your own boundaries and only doing things which you are happy to do is made possible through sexual consent.

A NOTE ON... Kink/Fetish

Students may raise the issue of fetishes and kink with you and how this relates to good sex / bad sex, pleasure and consent. Some of them will have read/ seen things like *Fifty Shades of Grey*. Others may have watched porn which features violence. Some may just be curious.

Concerns have been raised about topics like this being covered in RSE. However, if students have questions about this topic, it would not be helpful to dismiss them. By creating a safe space where questions can be asked without fear of judgement or taboo, students can begin to apply critical thinking to some of the content they or their classmates may have been exposed to. Failing to engage with students on more controversial topics can leave misinformation and dangerous narratives unchallenged and promote shame rather than empowerment.

The following scenario explains how a teacher could effectively deal with a conversation on this issue in an RSE lesson:

During the 'good sex / bad sex' lesson, as the teacher is taking whole class feedback and recording ideas on the board, one student offers 'spanking' as an example of good sex. Another student challenges this and says that spanking is abusive. The teacher thanks them both for their comments and explains that there is good reason for this difference of perspective. The teacher writes the word 'pain' in the middle, between good/bad. They recap what was said at the start of the activity about good/bad sex being subjective. They ask for ideas from the class about why, for many people, pain during sex would go on the bad side. Students offer things like pain is a barrier to pleasure, it could be degrading, it could be abusive and so on. The teacher then explains that, for a minority of people, they may regard certain painful acts to be sexually pleasurable. The teacher leads a discussion on what else would need to be present for this to be regarded as good sex for those people. Ideas include things like consent, empowerment, a safe word, compatibility, communication and so on. The teacher unpacks some of this with the class. What might empowerment entail and what could be a barrier to this? The teacher also highlights the fact that much of porn features more extreme sex acts. This can create the impression that minority sex acts are more common than they are (see more in Chapter 7).

A Further Note on Kink/Fetish

Students who watch porn may have come across videos which feature apparent or real pain being inflicted. Although some extreme adult porn is illegal, much of this genre is not. Porn featuring Bondage, Domination, Submission and Masochism (BDSM) is legally permissible as long as those who are hurt are not harmed.

Such content may give young people the impression that these are mainstream, standard sex acts. As will be discussed in Chapter 7, it is important to help students unpack the difference between fantasy and reality and apply critical thinking to what they are exposed to.

It is also important to note that porn stars engaged in this work are often experienced in giving/receiving such acts and that, in most cases, rules for engagement will have been thoroughly explored to ensure full consent and empowerment of all.

A Further, Further Note on Kink/Fetish

Not all kinks involve pain or violence. Whilst kink usually sits on the margins of sexual norms, there is a growing community of people who are bringing this to the mainstream. For some this is linked to queer sex, for others non-monogamy and so on. Often, this is conceived as a joyful, liberating movement based on a rejection of rigid socio-sexual norms.

Helping students to fully understand consent is the next step. Often, this is taught in negative terms, i.e., what rape is etc. This is important but will only be effective if students understand what consent actually looks like. In Chapter 3, inclusive case studies from popular TV shows were used as an example of how to achieve this.

Teaching what consent looks like should be done explicitly and repeated often. Shared language by all teachers and a stock explanation across all year groups will help to embed this messaging in students' thinking.

TEACHER TOOLKIT

What Does Consent Look Like?

1. Ask students to recap why consent is important and how it relates to the good sex / bad sex scales.

2. Ask groups to discuss the potential short- and long-term consequences of getting consent wrong – encourage them to think about the victim and perpetrator (i.e., that both can be damaged by this).

3. Ask groups to discuss: What does consent look like and how do we know we've got this right? Encourage students to think about what both people will be saying and doing with their bodies. E.g., 'does that feel good?', 'do you like this?', 'is this okay?'. Taking off their clothes, touching each other, etc.

4. Give the stock explanation:

   Consent involves both people ACTIVELY and WILLINGLY participating throughout the sexual encounter.

   Active = responsive, into it, saying yes (verbally and/or non-verbally), making positive noises, touching, moving, undressing.

   Willing = they want it! They understand what they're doing (not too drunk, too young or being coerced).

   Consent is a HELL YES!

   Before having sex, reflect on whether both of you will feel happy about this afterwards – 'is this what I want?', 'is this what my partner wants?', 'are we both going to feel happy about this in the morning?'

Consent is a FEEDBACK LOOP: Check in with your partner: 'Is this what you want?', 'does this feel good?', 'do you like that?', etc. Check in with yourself – are you happy with what's happening? Does it feel good? If not, try to speak up. Be as clear and assertive as you can.

Explain that consent is relevant and important for every person, regardless of their own gender or sexuality.

Explain that anyone can be a victim of sexual assault and whilst we can take measures to try to protect ourselves, this is not always possible. When sexual violence occurs, it is the fault and responsibility of the perpetrator, not the victim. It is important to be explicit about this to combat some of the pervading myths which perpetuate rape culture (explored below). What we can ensure is that we never cross the line and violate someone else. We can take full responsibility for our own actions when it comes to sex and always respect the agency of our future partner(s).

Recap the 'setting the tone' activity from Chapter 1: good sex vs bad sex. How will they ensure that they tip the scales in the right direction for themselves and their future partner(s)?

Most students will have identified that consent is the foundation of 'good sex' and that 'bad sex' often results from a violation of consent.

5. Self-reflection – How is this relevant to YOU? Consider sex, gender, sexuality. How might these be relevant? What does an empowered approach to sex look and feel like for you? How can you tap into and be attuned to your own needs and desires? How can you communicate this to a partner? Are there any potential barriers? How might these be overcome?

6. Discussion: What should you do if you are unsure if consent has been granted or if you perceive there to be a grey area? Allow some discussion of situations when this might occur, e.g., if people have been drinking a lot of alcohol or if they think they are getting mixed messages. If there is any perceived ambiguity or doubt, ask them how they should protect themselves and partner – by stopping. Clear communication is key. Remind them of the feedback loop of consent. Finish the lesson with a positive message that when two people are consenting this will be clear. Our aim is to empower students to understand what consent looks like and know how to get this right in practice.

A NOTE ON... Speaking Up

Whilst we want to encourage students to set boundaries and use their voices to communicate if they don't want something sexual, it is important to explain this is not always possible. If someone cannot speak up, this is not their fault.

Ask students to discuss why speaking up might be difficult. Tease out the possible factors. For example:

- They may fancy the other person and not want to upset them.

- They may have heard that sex should hurt and think this is normal.

- They may be experiencing coercive control and feel unable to speak.

- They may be too scared to say anything.

- They might freeze in the moment and want to say something but can't.

- They may be drunk and/or unconscious.

Discuss ways in which a person can try to find their voice, whilst acknowledging that this may not be possible. For example:

- Practise setting and communicating boundaries in all aspects of life.

- Discuss consent with your partner before you engage in sex. Discuss what you might like and making it clear that this might change. Ensure you have a shared understanding of what consent is and shared values about its importance.

- Ask your partner to check in with you in the moment.

- Understand what healthy and unhealthy relationships look like and be vigilant to 'red flags' (see Chapter 6).

- Check in with yourself – leading up to, during and after the sex act. Be attuned to how you are feeling, what you want and how you might communicate this.

- Perhaps have a specific word or sentence in mind that you will use if you need to.

Child-on-Child Sexual Abuse in Schools

Child-on-child sexual abuse in schools is nothing new but in 2021 entered public consciousness in a way that had never been seen before. The murder of Sarah Everard by MET police officer Wayne Cousins and the subsequent controversy surrounding the police's handling of a vigil in her memory sparked the biggest backlash against sexual violence since the #MeToo Movement of 2017. At around the same time, the online platform Everyone's Invited exploded with tens of thousands of testimonials of sexual abuse in British schools and universities. Against this backdrop, the Department for Education commissioned Ofsted to undertake an immediate review to investigate the scale of the problem.

Whilst the findings were unsurprising to many, they were shocking. Ofsted (2021) discovered that:

- Child-on-child sexual abuse is widespread in schools and considered normal by young people.
- Sexual harassment is pervasive in all contexts.
- Sexual harassment is often in the form of unsolicited nudes, with 90% of girls and 50% of boys being sent them 'a lot' / 'sometimes.'
- Misogynistic attitudes were pervasive with 92% of girls and 74% of boys witnessing sexist name calling 'a lot' / 'sometimes.'
- Teachers often underestimated the problem and were failing to prevent and address it effectively.
- Teachers lacked confidence in delivering the RSE curriculum related to sexual harassment and sexual violence, including online.
- Relationships and Sex Education was failing to give students the right information and advice in order to make the right choices.
- Schools and safeguarding partners were not closely aligned and did not fully understand the extent and significance of sexual harassment in schools or the local area.

Although consciousness has been raised, many schools still fail to prioritise RSE as a preventative measure, and many teachers still feel under-trained and -resourced and unsupported. This is a missed opportunity. Whilst studies on the efficacy of RSE have typically focused on sexual health outcomes, increasingly, recent studies have demonstrated the positive impact of RSE on:

Reducing abuse.
Reducing rape culture.
Increasing reporting of abuse.
Promoting gender equity and healthy relationships.

The Evidence

- In their review of three decades of RSE in schools, Goldfarb and Lieberman (2021) found a significant impact on reducing psychological, sexual and physical abuse perpetration. They also found that RSE is impactful in reducing attitudes which contribute to rape culture like victim blaming and acceptance of sexual coercion and harassment.

- A Cochrane Review (Walsh, 2015) found that 'children who are taught about preventing sexual abuse at school are more likely to tell an adult it they had, or were actually experiencing sexual abuse' (14 in 100, compared with four in 1,000).

- UNESCO (2018) cites potential effects of RSE in contributing to changes beyond health outcomes, including 'increasing gender equitable norms' and 'building stronger and healthier relationships.'

RSE provides an ongoing opportunity for students to acquire the knowledge, skills and self-awareness to be part of the solution to sexual violence and harassment between children. This is implicit in all RSE topics but also taught explicitly through the themes of:

- Setting and respecting boundaries.
- Healthy/ unhealthy relationships.
- Online interactions.
- Narratives from pornography.
- Misogyny.
- Sexual abuse, harassment and violence.
- Understanding sexual consent.
- Sexual pleasure and fulfilment.
- Communication.
- Self-awareness.
- Authenticity and character.

In addition to positive lessons on consent and healthy relationships, the reality of sexual abuse, the factors which contribute to it and the potential impact of such behaviours need to be explored.

TEACHER TOOLKIT

Understanding what can go wrong (as always, allow an opt-out and tell students ahead of the lesson that this will be covered).

The Law

Show the following scenarios and ask students to discuss if they think each is sexual harassment, sexual assault or rape:

1. Forcing someone to kiss you.

2. Telling sexually offensive jokes.

3. Lifting up someone's skirt.

4. Forcing a penis into someone's mouth whilst they're asleep.

5. Forcing someone to watch pornography.

6. Making sexual comments or jokes about someone's sexual orientation or gender reassignment.

7. Gesturing or making sexual remarks about someone's body, clothing or appearance.

8. Pressing up against another person for sexual pleasure.

9. Asking constant questions about someone's sex life.

10. A man pressuring a woman to have vaginal sex.

11. A man forcing a man to have anal sex.

12. A woman engaging in oral sex with another woman who is extremely drunk.

Go through the answers and definitions:

1. Assault.

2. Harassment.

3. Assault.

4. Rape.

5. Harassment.

6. Harassment.

7. Harassment.

8. Assault.

9. Harassment.

10. Rape.

11. Rape.

12. Assault.

Rape: When a person intentionally penetrates another's vagina, anus or mouth with a penis, without the other person's consent.

Sexual assault: Act of physical, psychological and emotional violation in the form of a sexual act, inflicted on someone without their consent. It can involve forcing or manipulating someone to witness or participate in any sexual acts. For example, unwanted kissing or touching, coercing someone into a sex act, revealing someone's genitals without their consent.

Sexual harassment: Unwanted behaviour of a sexual nature. For example, commenting on someone's body, asking questions about their sex life, continually asking someone on a date after they've said no, using a position of power to manipulate someone for sexual purposes.

Possible legal consequences:

Rape: Maximum prison sentence is life imprisonment.

All assault by penetration: Maximum sentence is life imprisonment.

Sexual assault: Maximum ten-year prison sentence.

Possession and distribution of Indecent Images of children: For possessing, the maximum is five years imprisonment, for distribution the maximum sentence is ten years.

All penetrative sex of a child aged 12 or younger is classified as rape: carries a maximum penalty of life imprisonment.

Sexual assault, causing or inciting a child under 13 to engage in sexual activity: Both carry a maximum sentence of 14 years in prison.

Sexual harassment in a school or workplace may be dealt with internally, e.g., by someone being suspended or through restorative practice. Sexual harassment becomes a crime and matter for the police in some specific cases, e.g., stalking, indecent exposure or 'upskirting.' The perpetrator may be charged and convicted. In some cases, the penalty may be prison (Rape Crisis, no date).

Using Case Studies

Ask students to discuss how consent is relevant to each of these examples. Note that these are not specific to particular genders/ sexualities.

- Someone receives an unsolicited image of a sexual nature.
- Someone is photographed or filmed without their knowledge.
- Someone sends an image of a sexual nature to a partner, and they share it with other people.
- Someone is having sex with a person who is very drunk.
- Two people are engaging in sex. One of them has their eyes open but they are not responding in any way.
- One person is saying no but they're laughing. They keep saying no but the other person keeps going.
- A person keeps being touched by someone else is an overly familiar way.
- Two people in a relationship have sex after one of them pressures the other to give in.
- Two people are having sex, and the person wearing the condom removes it then continues having sex without the other person realising.

Also consider using case studies from the Everyone's Invited testimonials. Use these to further tease out the themes already explored: Who is at fault? How could things have been handled differently? What short- and long-term consequences might this have on the victim and perpetrator?

Rape Culture

- Starter:
  - Look at the following scenario and ask groups to discuss various points where blame can be apportioned:
    - A 17-year-old girl goes to a party with her 29-year-old boyfriend. The girl has a reputation for sleeping around. She has not had

sex with her boyfriend although she's told him that she will soon. She has even bought some condoms which she keeps in her purse. She's worn her new dress to the party which is very short. Over the course of the night, she drinks a lot of alcohol until she is babbling incoherently and slipping in and out of consciousness. Whilst she's in this state her boyfriend has sex with her.

- ○ Can any evidence of victim blaming / rape culture be found in the students' responses?

- ○ Make it clear that this scenario depicts a scene of rape. There is one rapist and one victim. The only person at fault is the rapist.

- ○ Most rapes happen when the rapist is known to the victim.

- ○ Explain that many people argue that there is a 'grey area' when it comes to sexual consent but this simply is not the case. Show the video *Tea Consent (Clean)* (Blue Seat Studios, 2015). This can easily be found online.

- ○ Explain that it is unsurprising that some placed blame on her (no judgement). We have all been socialised to do this, but this is rape culture, and we are going to unpack and challenge this.

- Discussion: What do you understand by the term 'rape culture'?

- Definition: Rape culture is:

- ○ Social trends which legitimise, tolerate or even glamorise sexual violence towards women.

- ○ When 'victim' is redefined as 'slut.'

- ○ Rape jokes.

- ○ Rape threats.

- ○ Slut shaming and double standards.

- ○ The impression that all men are sex crazed and cannot control their desires.

- ○ A disproportionate focus on false accusations.

- Discuss examples:

- ○ The song and music video for "Blurred Lines."

- ○ Adverts which objectify women's bodies.

- ○ Narratives/genres in porn, e.g., 'gang bang.'

- ○ Examples of rape jokes.

- ○ Examples of rape threats from social media.

- ○ Newspaper articles with victim blaming. For example, in the year 2012–13 the *Daily Mail* used the phrase 'cried rape' in 54 headlines (Rape Crisis Scotland, 2021).

- ○ Examples of court cases where the victim's sexual history is used to discredit them.

- ○ Explain: these are all pieces of a puzzle which contribute to the socialised message that women are objects, male desire is uncontrollable and that women are somehow asking for rape.

- Put this in context – we have a problem:

  - ○ Nine in ten schoolgirls say sexist name calling and unsolicited nudes are commonplace for them or girls they know.

  - ○ One in four women have been raped or sexually assaulted as an adult.

  - ○ One in six children have been sexually abused.

  - ○ One in 20 men have been raped or sexually assaulted as an adult.

  - ○ The highest-ever number of rapes within a 12-month period was recorded in the year ending March 2022: 70,330. In that same period, charges were brought in just 2,223 rape cases (Rape Crisis England and Wales, 2022).

- A woman is killed by a man every three days in the UK (Femicide census, 2020).

Rape Culture in Action – Case Study: Steubenville High

In 2012, a 16-year-old Steubenville High pupil (female) was raped by two boys at a party. As she lay drunk and unconscious, they dragged her around by her feet, offered to pay people to urinate on her, raped her and filmed their crime. They then shared the video around their friends.

The reaction from peers was to blame her. They called her a slut and a skank and said nobody liked her anyway.

The reaction from the court – one- and two-year sentences (the longer sentence for the boy who filmed it).

The reaction from the media – sympathy with the perpetrators, rather than the victim. Show the now infamous CNN clip from outside the courthouse after the verdicts were read out: "These two young men had such promising futures; star football players, very good students. They watched as their lives fell apart."

The reaction from Serena Williams - "She shouldn't have put herself in that position" ... "Do you think it's fair, what they got?" (Sherwin, 2013). She later apologised and reached out to the victim.

The reaction on Twitter (a selection of many tweets criticising the victim):

"Be responsible for your decisions ladies before your drunken decisions ruin innocent lives."

"Has anyone considered that the girl might just be a slut? Surely if she hadn't consented nothing would have happened…"

"I feel bad for the two young guys."

"They did what most people in their situation would have done."

"… this girl sounds like a slut that got drunk had sex with two dudes on the same night regretted it, cried rape."

"That's not rape, you're just a loose, drunk slut."

(cited in Dunne, 2017).

… This is rape culture.

After sharing this example with students, ask for their response to each of the reactions. What is going on here? What social factors may have contributed to this? Is this rape culture?

- You might want to use the BBC documentary 'Is This Rape?' to explore this further.

  ○ Recap the definition of sexual consent.

  ○ Show the first part of the film up to the point where the young people are asked if Gemma consented.

  ○ Ask your students to anonymously vote - Did Gemma consent - yes/no/unsure.

  ○ Show the voting and results on the video.

  ○ Compare your results with theirs. You will probably observe a big difference - i.e., that your students have all or mostly voted 'no.' This is because you have given them a clear definition of consent. Ask them to discuss what they think about the responses in the video.

○ The documentary continues, but this part is the most useful.

○ Reflect – this is a heterosexual example. Discuss how this could happen with people of different genders and sexualities.

○ Discuss – how can every one of us protect ourselves from crossing the line in the way that Tom did in the video?

Signposting Support for Victims

○ Consider medical help.

○ Consider reporting (don't change/wash clothes).

○ Call 111, visit 111 online or go to a 24-hour sexual health referral centre, your GP surgery, A&E or a genitourinary medicine (GUM) / sexual health clinic.

○ Seek support from a voluntary organisation, such as Rape Crisis, Women's Aid, Victim Support, The Survivors Trust or Male Survivors Partnership.

○ Call the 24-hour freephone National Domestic Abuse Helpline, run by Refuge, on 0808 2000 247 or the Rape Crisis national freephone helpline on 0808 802 9999.

○ Go to the police if you feel able.

○ Talk to a friend or family member.

○ Support in school (remind students about the limits of confidentiality).

○ The NSPCC's Report Abuse in Education helpline can be contacted by calling 0800 136 663, or emailing help@nspcc.org.uk.

How to Support a Victim

○ Listen to what they want to tell you. Don't ask for extra details. Don't ask why they didn't make it stop.

○ Don't make it about you and your emotional response.

○ Tell them you believe them.

○ Offer to help them go to the police/hospital, etc. without putting pressure on them to do so.

- ○ Ask them if they want you to talk to their parents on their behalf. Respect their decision.

- ○ They might not want to be touched, so be mindful of this when offering them a hug.

- ○ If you are in a sexual relationship with the victim, understand that sex with you may be triggering. Give them time and understanding.

A NOTE ON… **A Whole-School Approach**

KCSIE (2023) states that a whole-school or college approach to safeguarding should:

- Promote a zero-tolerance approach which makes it clear that sexual violence and sexual harassment is never acceptable and will not be tolerated.

- Provide a strong preventative education programme.

Whilst RSE is one of the greatest tools schools have to prevent child-on-child sexual abuse and harassment, this will be made most effective against the backdrop of a whole-school approach.

The following pillars of a whole-school preventative approach can help to plan and embed your school's commitment.

1. Commit to making this a priority:

   - ○ Lead from the top and be unambiguous in your school's commitment.

   - ○ Ensure all staff see active prevention as their duty.

   - ○ Prioritise curriculum time for RSE.

   - ○ Invest in regular whole-staff training (including of governors), specialist RSE training and external speakers to complement your RSE lessons.

   - ○ Invest in your RSE lead – give them the time, status and pay commensurate with this whole-school role.

2. Commit to lasting change:

   - ○ Evaluate how data is recorded and trends monitored.

- ○ Increase your data monitoring – not just recording incidents but also monitoring student attitudes.

- ○ Acknowledge problems at your school.

- ○ Regularly gather data to monitor the efficacy of your initiatives.

- ○ Adopt a multi-agency approach to monitor local trends and share resources.

- ○ Value student voice, and ask students to help shape your strategic responses.

3. Commit to a shared philosophy:

- ○ Embed this commitment in your school values and strategic aims.

- ○ Articulate and enforce a zero-tolerance approach to sexual abuse.

- ○ Combine zero tolerance with restorative approaches.

- ○ Ensure that every member of staff understands and reinforces the same approach.

- ○ Ensure that staff model and promote gender equity.

- ○ Commit to Equity, Diversity, and Inclusion throughout all aspects of school life.

- ○ Engage parents as much as possible through consultations, information evenings and newsletters.

To reinforce the messaging to challenge rape culture, it is useful to reflect on what is happening in your school more broadly and to ensure that rape culture is not being perpetuated by teachers / the school culture. Consider:

- Messages around school uniform / non-school uniform days?

- Language like 'ladylike,' 'modesty,' 'reputation'?

- Messages around sexual attitudes and behaviours?

- Assumptions about gender and sexuality?

- Victim blaming?

- If rape culture is effectively challenged?

- Gendered stereotypes?

- Complacency?

CASE STUDY: School Uniform

School X is a traditional co-ed school which has always valued the importance of school uniform and school reputation.

However, female students reported that the staff's enforcing of the uniform rules made them feel sexualised and shamed. Comments about girls' modesty and public examination of their skirt length were cited as examples, in addition to some comments about the distraction they may be causing to male students and staff.

In response, the school did the following:

- 'Girl' and 'boy' uniforms were replaced with 'skirt' and 'trouser' options, available to everyone.

- All staff were given training on rape culture and misogyny.

- Staff were given crib sheets on how to challenge uniform and phrases to avoid.

Students were consulted in all the above.

TROUBLESHOOTING… Defensiveness from Boys

Lessons on consent can run the risk of alienating boys by engendering a sense of defensiveness. Some boys have described experiencing these lessons as an attack, feeling that they are being blamed for the crimes of others. Although it can be frustrating for a teacher to experience this response, it is essential that we engage boys effectively, or we will not be effective in combatting sexual violence.

'Not All Men'

'Not all men' was a phrase which kept appearing as the #MeToo Movement gained traction. In some cases, this was men who perceived themselves to be 'good men' and wanted to distance themselves from the behaviour of others. At other times, this was a blatant challenge to the droves of women describing (in many cases for the first time) their experiences of rape and sexual violence. "But it's not ALL men!" When #NotAllMen began trending on social media, many of the posts attempted to diminish the extent of and damage caused by sexual violence. Rather than ask how men could help, many of the posts adopted a sense of victimhood for men and further attacked women, feminism and victims of sexual violence.

The sentiments of #NotAllMen remain online, in what is sometimes referred to as the 'Manosphere'. In her book *Men Who Hate Women* (2021), Laura Bates charts the rise of extreme online misogyny including Incels (Involuntary Celibates) and MGTOW (Men Going Their Own Way). She cautions that many young men are becoming radicalised by a seductive narrative which paints men as the victims of a woke world which only values crazy, man-hating women. Rapists, murderers of women and misogynists like Andrew Tate are glorified as heroes who are finally bringing women back under male control.

A NOTE ON... Andrew Tate

At the time of writing, Andrew Tate, whose hashtag has received over 13 billion views on TikTok (Oppenheim, 2023) is awaiting trial on rape and trafficking charges in Romania. Tate's huge popularity seems to be linked to his persona as a successful, physically strong alpha male who speaks his mind. Many of his posts feature sports cars and kick boxing and his fans see him as a charismatic hero. His critics, however, regard him as a danger-ous misogynist, propagating hate speech and causing damage to society. Tate regards women as men's property. He advocates men having multiple wives and condemns promiscuous women as "disgusting." He has argued that rape victims should bear some responsibility and brags about hitting and choking women. Quotes like "It's bang out the machete, boom in her face and grip her by the neck. Shut up bitch," leave little ambiguity about the way he believes women should be treated. Indeed, he calls women "dumb hoes" and claims to only date women aged 18-19 so he can "make an imprint on them" (Das, 2022). Tate has made a fortune from his huge online following.

Many teachers have understandably become concerned about the popularity of Andrew Tate amongst boys, and attempts have been made to address this in schools. However, as well intentioned as these attempts can be, they can run the risk of polarising views within the classroom and in turn embed a sense of tribalism amongst boys. When this happens, it is likely to create a sense of defensiveness, making discussions combative, thus likely undermining the intent of the lesson. Even for boys who do not idolise Tate, many of them regard him as a joke. By focusing on Tate exclusively, the teacher and the lesson can lose all credibility.

When discussing online misogyny, the following approaches are likely to be more effective:

- Avoid naming Tate yourself. Instead, focus on multiple sources of online misogyny. Help students to apply critical thinking to everything they view, not just posts by or about Tate.

- If students mention Tate, acknowledge why some people find him appealing, e.g., challenging authority, engaging social media, lifestyle advice, appealing to those who feel let down by society and offering simple solutions to complex problems. Avoid condemnation or judgement. Instead, facilitate a classroom culture of curiosity and growth. Ask students to think about why some people are concerned and what is happening more broadly in terms of sexual violence, etc. Is it possible there's a link? How does this relate to the broader picture of misogyny on and offline? Try to find the nuance, and encourage empathy and critical thinking.

- Use evidence, rather than rhetoric, to highlight the impact of misogyny. For example, one rape happens in schools every school day in the UK on average (Bates, 2022). Ask students to identify for themselves what factors may be contributing to this shocking problem.

- Include discussions on misogyny within broader discussions about prejudice and discrimination.

- Include discussions on misogyny within broader discussions about social media and how to apply critical thinking skills, for example, by discussing algorithms, echo chambers and filter bubbles.

- Use RSE lessons to lay the implicit foundations of anti-misogyny before explicitly addressing this. For example, through lessons on consent, healthy relationships and porn. The safe space of an RSE classroom, where students can ask questions and have discussions is likely to have a more positive impact than an assembly.

- As a school, adopt a zero-tolerance approach to misogynistic behaviour but combine this with restorative approaches which promote a culture of growth and curiosity.

TROUBLESHOOTING

Although most boys will not be immersed in the 'manosphere,' many of them will have been exposed to online misogyny. It is, therefore, crucial that lessons on sexual violence are handled very skilfully.

Beginning lessons on sexual violence by acknowledging that it is not all men can help with this. Stating this explicitly before it is named by students gives you the opportunity to set the tone, address any concerns or misconceptions and help boys to see that they are not being attacked. Against this backdrop, it can then be established that whilst not all men/boys are perpetrators of sexual violence, pretty much all women/girls have been sexually harassed, abused or assaulted. It is not all men, but we have to acknowledge that the perpetrators of sexual violence (around 98%) are, almost always, men (Rape Crisis England and Wales, 2022).

False rape accusations:

Many boys are concerned about the prevalence of false rape accusations, and this can, for some, be a far greater concern than sexual violence itself. This is a topic often discussed on social media and can be a barrier to the message you are trying to deliver.

It is, therefore, a good idea to address this early on to avoid it being a reason to dismiss what's being discussed.

Firstly, it is important to acknowledge that false accusations do happen, and they are abhorrent and illegal. Victims of this can have their reputations, careers and lives destroyed.

However, it is then important to put this in context:

- False rape accusations are extremely rare. In 2018, Channel 4 conducted a detailed investigation, using robust national statistics, and found that the average adult man in England and Wales has a 0.0002% chance of being falsely accused of rape in a year (Bates, 2021).

- A false rape accusation is unlikely to lead to prosecution, and the accused is legally presumed innocent unless the guilt is proven in a court of law. Even in legitimate rape cases, only 1.6% result in a criminal charge. Some people argue that rape has effectively been decriminalised in this country – this injustice affects tens of thousands more people every year in this country than false rape accusations (Bates, 2021).

- A man in the UK is 230 times more likely to be raped himself than be falsely accused of rape (Bates, 2021). Therefore, whilst false rape accusations are terrible, a far greater risk is male sexual violence and that will be the focus of the remaining lessons on consent.

- In most cases, when someone says they've been raped, they have. A disproportionate focus on false rape accusations can run the risk of diverting our attention from the problem of sexual violence. It can reinforce the idea that victims are lying or somehow deserved what happened to them. It may make victims less likely to report the crime, juries less likely to find rapists guilty and embolden those who want to commit such acts. If we want to live in a society where victims of sexual violence can seek justice, we must first acknowledge the scale of the problem. This is not an attack on all men. It is a plea for all men to be part of the solution.

Only men can rape:

Some boys may feel affronted by the fact that in UK law rape can only be committed by someone with a penis. They may see this as anti-male bias and unfair. However, sexual assault by penetration (which can be committed by any gender) carries the same maximum term of life in prison.

Winning boys over:

The above strategies will help to anticipate and prevent some of the issues which can arise. In addition to this, try the following:

- Celebrate boys. Some boys feel that girls are treated favourably in school and this can make them less receptive to messages combatting misogyny and lessons on consent. Whilst there are good reasons for International Women's Day receiving more attention than Men's Day, perhaps consider how you might use events like this to celebrate boys for their good character. Create opportunities to give boys leadership roles to overcome their sense of alienation. Create opportunities to listen to boys and avoid dismissing them.

- Supporting boys emotionally. Boys sometimes feel that girls get more emotional support than they do. For example, if a heterosexual couple break up, the girls' friends may rally around them, and teachers offer support and adjustments. There can be an assumption that boys are fine if they are not showing their emotions publicly. Make an extra effort to be aware of this, then explicitly combat any perception that they have been left behind. Some boys are concerned about the rising rate in suicidal ideation and completion and can feel that schools are not taking this seriously. Explore this in lessons and acknowledge gendered factors in mental health. Help boys to see that they are seen, heard and supported.

- A useful addition to your lessons can be using peer-to-peer engagement where older boys speak to younger boys. The older students gain insight into why these lessons are needed (as they hear some of the comments from younger boys), and younger boys are more likely to engage. Importantly, this can help to overcome the sense of tribalism that can emerge where boys feel under attack and so withdraw from the whole process. Instead, we can empower boys to lead this work and help us to understand how they can be part of the solution.

TEACHER TOOLKIT

Recap Learning

Questions for discussion:

1. Define consent.

2. What kinds of things might indicate a lack of consent?

3. Who can be a victim of sexual assault?

4. In what kinds of situations is sexual assault most common?

5. Who is at fault?

6. Why is it important for you to get sexual consent right? How can you empower yourself to do this?

7. How does sexual pleasure link to sexual consent?

Answers to draw out:

1. Consent requires both active and willing participation in sex. To be willing you need to understand what you're agreeing to. You cannot do this when drunk.

2. Saying 'no', zero response, looking uncomfortable, too drunk / on drugs, jokingly saying 'please don't' etc.

3. Anyone. Female, male, gay, straight, etc. Sexual predators are most commonly heterosexual men.

4. When the victim is known to the perpetrator.

5. The perpetrator only.

6. Understand consent. Check in with your partner. Avoid sex with anyone who's drunk. If in doubt, wait. If you're uncomfortable, try to speak up. Don't ever cross the line!

7. Know what you want and deserve and how to ask for it. If it doesn't feel good, speak up if you can.

6 Recognising Healthy and Unhealthy Relationships

Recognising healthy and unhealthy relationships is, for many, a lifelong pursuit. The work we do in the classroom can help our students to work out what they want to bring to and get from future relationships. An empowering approach is one which:

- Builds self-awareness.
- Promotes agency.
- Develops compassion.
- Is linked to character education.
- Builds resilience.
- Emphasises growth over perfection.
- Focuses as much on healthy relationships as unhealthy relationships.

A NOTE ON... **Character Education**

Although the statutory framework is focused on Relationships, Sex and Health Education, most schools will deliver this as part of a broader PSHE programme. Having Character Education as a thread which runs across this is a good way of ensuring meaningful, lifelong engagement from students. In Chapter 3 we discussed the unique lens through which each of our students will approach the lessons and the importance of helping them see the relevance to themselves. In addition to this, emphasis on character encourages students to ask themselves:

- What are my values?
- Who do I admire?

DOI: 10.4324/9781003437932-7

- What kind of person do I want to be?

- What are my red lines?

- Are my behaviours aligned with my principles?

Rather than simply teaching facts to be regurgitated, our lessons are about empowering young people with life skills, a keen sense of self and the ability to reflect on their behaviours and make choices which are right for them.

Laying the Foundations

Before getting into teaching romantic/sexual relationships, it is useful to lay some broader foundations around self-esteem, boundaries and friendships. Empowering students to build strong self-esteem, set healthy boundaries and build positive non-sexual relationships will all make later lessons more impactful.

TEACHER TOOLKIT

Laying the Foundations

The following activities could be used with Year 7/8. Used in sequence, these help students think about their role in relationships and the power they have over the choices they make.

Building Self-Esteem

- What does low self-esteem look like? What do people say to themselves when they feel bad about themselves? Ask students to write statements on post-it notes and stick these on one side of the white board. They may need some guidance with this. Statements might include things like 'I am ugly,' 'I am stupid,' 'nobody likes me,' 'I am worthless,' 'I am a bad person,' 'I am a failure,' etc.

- What does strong self-esteem look like? What do we say to ourselves when we feel good about ourselves? Ask students to write statements on post-it notes and stick these on the other side of the board. They may need some guidance with this. Statements might include things like 'I am a good person,' I like myself,' 'I like how I look,' 'I know that failure is a normal part of life,' 'I am good enough,' 'I am worthy,' 'I am loveable,' 'people like me,' etc.

- Read out both sides as a class. Explain that throughout our lives we can move between both sides. We want to empower them with the skills to build their self-esteem now and in the future.

- Group discussion: What factors might contribute to low self-esteem? E.g., critical parents, critical teachers, critical friends, no self-belief, low resilience, prone to giving up, fixed mindset, pessimistic, etc. Ask how these thoughts can influence feelings and emotions. Feelings might include anger, hopelessness, disgust, loneliness and envy. Behaviours might include isolating yourself, accepting unhealthy relationships, unhealthy behaviours and refusal to take risks.

- Group discussion: What factors might contribute to strong self-esteem? E.g., supportive parents, supportive teachers, supportive friends, resilience, perseverance, growth mindset, optimistic, etc. Ask how these thoughts can influence feelings and emotions. Feelings might include secure, at peace, hopeful, connected to others, stable and happy. Behaviours might include trying new challenges, meeting new people and building positive relationships.

- Get feedback as a class, and help students tease out which factors we might have some control over. Ask students to begin to put together some strategies for building strong self-esteem. Explain that, whilst there are many factors outside of our control, each of us can set intentions, build skills and practise strategies to strengthen our self-esteem and sense of empowerment.

- Share some strategies:

  ○ Try to work out your principles and live by them. This will help to build self-respect.

  ○ Try not to let other people's judgement define you.

  ○ Understand your strengths and weaknesses. None of us are perfect, and accepting this about yourself can be powerful. If we only focus on our strengths and achievements, this can make failure really difficult to take.

  ○ Put yourself out there. Try new challenges, meet new people, express yourself. The more you do this, the more your confidence will build.

  ○ Try not to judge others. Putting others down is often a sign of insecurity. People with strong self-esteem lift others up. This also helps us to strengthen our sense of character. When we do good things, we feel good about ourselves.

○ Surround yourself with the right people. People who champion your achievements but also challenge you when needed.

○ Challenge negative thinking traps:

Look back at the board with statements on low self-esteem. Explain that each of us can become trapped in negative thinking patterns. It can feel like this though is truth/fact when really it is the result of low self-esteem rather than reality. For example:

Alex worries that he doesn't have enough friends in his new school and that nobody likes him. He's been hanging around with a new group outside of school. When he hears them making a racist joke, he laughs along with them even though he finds it offensive. Later on, he makes a racist comment himself and everyone laughs.

What is going on for Alex?

Existing belief: Nobody likes him.

Evidence that supports this belief: He's in a new school and doesn't have many friends.

Impact of this belief: He is so desperate for friends he's picking the wrong people. His behaviour does not match his values: this may become a barrier to him making better friendships, and his self-esteem may get even lower as a result.

How can Alex challenge this thinking trap?

New belief: People do like me. I will make friends. I deserve good friends.

Evidence that supports this belief: He had friends in the past; it takes time to build friendships; he gets on with lots of people.

Now Alex has chosen a new belief, what can he practically do with this? Take his time, choose to be around people he really likes, and build friendships with people he enjoys being around.

Ask students to privately answer the same questions, this time on a negative thinking trap they experience:

What is going on for you?

Existing belief:

Evidence that supports this belief:

Impact of this belief:

How can you challenge this thinking trap?

New belief:

Now you have chosen a new belief, what can you practically do with this?

Linking to Friendships

Helping students to work out what kind of friend they want to be and what kinds of friends they want to have is an excellent place to start in helping them to recognise healthy and unhealthy relationships.

Baseline activity: What do you deserve from relationships? Ask students to draw themselves in the centre of a page and record what they deserve in all kinds of relationships, e.g., trust, safety and kindness. They can revisit this throughout the lesson/course and add new ideas.

Discussion:

Friendships –

- What's great?

- What can be tricky?

- What's happening around your age that might put some pressure on friendships?

Toxic friendships –

What are they?

How do you know you're in one?

What are the warning signs you might be in a toxic friendship? E.g.:

- They have crossed a major boundary for you, with no apologies.

- Instead of communicating that something is wrong, they make passive-aggressive comments.

- They are jealous of you/your other friendships.

- They insult you or are mean to you.

- They try to humiliate you.

- ○ You can't seem to do anything right by them.

Scenarios: Ask students to look at each and come up with some advice.

- You've been best friends since Year 3, but now your friend has started ignoring you.

- Everyone has been invited to a party except you.

- All your friends are on a WhatsApp group but won't let you in.

- You keep being added to a WhatsApp group you don't want to be in.

- Boundaries:

Discuss: What are boundaries and why might these be important?

Physical: Personal space; who we allow to touch us – where and how.

Emotional: How we allow others to make us feel.

Sexual: What we are comfortable doing / not doing, details we want to share / not share.

Relationships: Behaviour we are willing / not willing to be around.

Time: What we are / are not willing to spend our time on.

Setting boundaries:

Role play:

Your friend keeps coming to your house unexpectedly. They have bought loads of the same clothes as you and they are messaging you constantly. You are finding them very needy. You want things to change but you don't want to lose them as a friend.

Act this out and find a way of setting boundaries.

Share good examples.

Setting your own boundaries.

Link back to self-esteem and the thinking traps. Remind students of the importance of building strong self-esteem and using this as a basis for positive relationships.

In romantic/sexual relationships ask yourself: Do you want this? Do you feel empowered? Do you feel safe? Do you feel respected? Do you feel able to share what you really think?

If not, what could you say?

Suggestions:

'I'm not comfortable with this.'

'Please respect my boundaries.'

'I've told you no, and I mean it.'

'I don't want this.'

Do:

Talk to a trusted adult.

Consider ending a relationship if the other person will not respect your boundaries.

Report any problems.

Love Yourself – if someone violates your consent it's not your fault, it's theirs.

Violating Boundaries

Look at each of the scenarios below and discuss how this relates to boundaries:

1) A boy pulls down another boy's pants in front of everyone in the changing room.

2) A girl walks up to a boy and grabs him between the legs.

3) A girl tells everyone who her best mate has snogged.

4) A boy grabs a girl's breast in the school corridor.

5) A girl pressures her girlfriend to go to bed with her.

6) A boy finds out another boy is gay and tells everyone.

Scenarios 1, 2 and 4 are examples of sexual assault. We need to use this language and call it out.

Scenarios 3 and 6 are betrayals of trust. What motivates this betrayal? What might the consequences be? Is this okay? Scenario 5 is an example of sexual coercion.

Sometimes it can be difficult to speak up. Sometimes it can be difficult to seek help. Emphasise what power we do have: Know that you deserve to be treated well; identify and share your own boundaries; respect other people's boundaries.

Linking to Relationships

Share the famous quote by Ru Paul: "If you can't love yourself, how the hell you gonna love somebody else?" Ask for some reflections on this. How might strong/low self-esteem affect relationships? Tease out the idea that strong self-esteem is a good foundation for healthy relationships, e.g., believing you deserve to be treated well, choosing someone who is kind to you, ending an abusive relationship and treating your partner with care and respect.

Healthy Romantic and Sexual Relationships

Helping students to recognise the features of a healthy relationship is incredibly important but sometimes neglected. Healthy relationships are more than an absence of abuse. They provide an opportunity for human connection, mutual growth, the foundation of a family and so much more. A skills- and character-based approach will help students to navigate the nuances of relationships and continue to build on their learning throughout their lives. When students reflect on their own values and principles regarding relationships, they begin to identify their hopes, what they want to avoid and the type of partner they want to be. This promotes a sense of agency and responsibility as they begin their relationships.

TEACHER TOOLKIT

What Do We Want from Relationships?

Discuss: In what ways can romantic relationships be positive and/or negative forces in our lives?

Diamond Nine Activity

Issue nine cards with the text below to pairs. Ask them to discuss and rank the cards. They can add three more cards with other ideas. Discuss.

Good Looking	Funny	Wants to spend time with me
Lust	Someone I can trust	Gets on well with my friends
Can show how they feel	Someone who's really into me	Love

Beginning Relationships

Ask students to look at the case-study cards below. Discuss:

Where have things gone well and why?

Which scenarios have gone badly? What advice would you give? How does this relate to your values?

James and Sam met in their first week of college. They quickly became friends and began going to the gym together. James realised he really liked Sam but wasn't sure if he felt the same. He thought Sam might be flirting with him, but he was finding it difficult to read the signs. Eventually he asked Sam if he'd like to go bowling. Sam agreed and whilst they were there the conversation flowed easily and James felt confident that Sam might fancy him. He asked Sam if he was in a relationship and they both made it clear that they were single. James asked Sam if he would like to go out again and if he would consider this as a date. Sam said he'd love that and after several dates James asked Sam to be his boyfriend. He agreed.

When Rob joined Sarah's school in Year 9, she knew she fancied him straight away. They sat next to each other in Maths and over time, Sarah felt a connection building. Sarah told all her friends about this and asked one of them to let Rob know she fancied him. Her friends told her that Rob looked really embarrassed and didn't respond, so Sarah sent him a Snapchat telling him she liked him. Rob still didn't respond. Eventually, Sarah found out that Rob was going out with one of her friends, so she started spreading rumours about them cheating on each other. In Maths she started calling him 'gay' and laughing at him. Sarah has hated Rob ever since.

Mo and Rose go to different schools. They have mutual friends but have never met in person. They have followed each other on Instagram and started chatting. Over time, it's clear that they both like each other (more than friends) and they decide to meet in person. The meeting makes them realise there's definitely something there. They keep chatting online and meeting up, and eventually Rose asks if they should make their relationship official. Mo explains that he wants to take things slowly. Rose is disappointed but accepts his decision. They continue as they are for a few weeks but begin to drift apart. They haven't chatted since.

Caleb and Izzy had known each other since nursery. They had never been close friends, but by the time they were in Year 10, Caleb started developing feelings for Izzy. One day, he told her he fancied her in front of everyone. Izzy was clearly embarrassed and didn't know what to say. Everyone else seemed to find it funny when Caleb started stroking her leg and speaking in a sexual way about her. Later that evening, Caleb surprised Izzy by turning up at her house and telling her he wanted to go out with her. Izzy explained that she liked him but did not want to go out with him. They agreed to just be friends but, when Caleb went home, he sent her lots of messages telling her she was beautiful and begging her to go out with him.

Vix and Charlie met at a party one night. They were immediately drawn to each other and spent the whole evening laughing and chatting. As the party came to an end, they went off with their separate friendship groups and both regretted not having kissed. Vix couldn't stop thinking about Charlie and eventually got her Snap details from a mutual friend. They began chatting and although it was awkward at first, they agreed to meet in person the following weekend. They found that the conversation started flowing easily again, and Vix confessed that she regretted not having kissed Charlie at the party. Charlie asked if she still wanted to and when she said yes, they started kissing.

Dealing with Relationship Issues

There is some subjectivity when it comes to healthy/unhealthy relationships. Helping students to acquire their own sense of self and values will help them to work out for themselves what is important. All relationships will face some problems and they will need to work out what they are willing to tolerate and what they are not. Of course, with life experience, this may evolve over time. Ask students to consider the following scenarios. Are these red lines, fine or are they unsure?

You've been in a relationship for a few months and you have introduced your partner to your friends and family. The problem is, they never introduce you to their friends or family. You're starting to worry about what's going on.

You have been in a relationship for some time and your partner wants to have sex but you don't feel ready. They are putting lots of pressure on you. You really like them but you're worried they'll dump you if you keep saying no.

You have been in a relationship for some time and you want to have sex but your partner isn't ready.

You catch your partner watching porn.

You have sex with your partner for the first time and they tell you they have sorted out contraception and not to worry. Afterwards you realise they were lying and did not use any protection.

You go to have sex for the first time with your partner and neither of you have contraception. You both really want to go ahead and your partner is willing to risk it.

Your partner gets on really well with your best friend. Whenever they are together, they laugh and joke with each other and you begin to feel jealous.

You introduce your partner to your friends, and it doesn't go well. Your friends have some big concerns about your relationship.

Your partner has been reading your text messages and getting very possessive over you. You think it's because they love you so much, but it's beginning to feel suffocating.

You have sex for the first time with your partner, and they tell all of your mutual friends all of the details of what happened.
You are in a sexual relationship, and your partner is getting lots of sexual pleasure, but you are not.
You are in a sexual relationship, and you are getting lots of sexual pleasure, but your partner is not.
Either you or your partner are experiencing pain during sex.
You send a sexual image of yourself to your partner. They promise to keep it private but share it with their friends.
You are in a relationship but realise you are no longer attracted to your partner. You start fancying someone else and have the opportunity to be unfaithful with them.
Your partner cheats on you.
Your partner suggests that you have an open relationship. They want you to be able to stay together but see other people too.
Your partner tells you they don't fancy you.

Ending a Relationship

Go to YouTube and show '100 People Tell Us About Their Worst Breakup' by Cut (2019) www.youtube.com/watch?v=RfxU4GE4vWM

Discussion Task

- What are some of the worst ways to break up a relationship?

- What are some of the best ways to break up a relationship?

- What are some of the worst ways to deal with a break-up?

- What are some of the best ways to deal with a break-up and get over the end of a relationship? Why can this be so difficult?

Reflection: How will you ensure that your character and values are reflected in the way you:

- Start relationships.

- Conduct yourself during a relationship.

- End relationships.

Unhealthy Relationships

Once students have reflected on the features of healthy relationships, the work on unhealthy relationships can begin. This can be a tricky and potentially triggering topic to engage with. Some students may be living in homes where unhealthy relationships have been modelled all their lives. Some may be in an unhealthy relationship themselves. As always, prepare students for what you are covering ahead of the lesson, be vigilant to safeguarding concerns and adopt a non-judgemental approach.

These lessons will give students knowledge of the features of unhealthy relationships and how to access support. They will begin to acquire a keen sense of self and the skills to choose and contribute to healthy relationships.

TEACHER TOOLKIT

Red Flags

Issue students with the case-study cards below.

What's going on here?

Is this a problem?

What advice would you give?

Case study 1	Case study 2
You have been with your partner for several months. You get on really well and want to spend as much time with them as possible. Gradually, you spend less time with your friends but, when your best friend's birthday comes along, you're really looking forward to their party. Leading up to this, your partner tells you that they don't trust your best friend and asks you not to go. You have a big argument about this, and your partner gives you an ultimatum: choose them or your best friend.	You and your partner are in love. When things are going well it's great, but you find that you keep arguing and the arguments are becoming more frequent and intense. Your partner gets very jealous when you speak to other people and keeps accusing you of cheating on them. To stop you going to a party they lock you in the house. They apologise afterwards but next time you want to go out things get physical and they push you back in the house when you try to leave.

Case Study 3	Case Study 4
Your partner is very critical of you. You're sure they love you, but they keep making negative comments about your appearance and personality. They've told you they hate your long hair and want you to cut it. When you refuse, they come up behind you and cut a chunk off your hair. They laugh this off and say it's a joke. After you go and get your hair cut, they buy you flowers.	You arrange for your partner to meet your parents for the first time. You're feeling nervous but excited, and your parents have prepared a meal. After they're more than an hour late you call your partner, and they say they forgot all about it. This isn't the first time they've let you down. Each time they blame you for being unclear about the plans.

Types of Abuse

Ask for definitions of the following: Domestic abuse, coercive control, harassment, sexual exploitation. Share the definitions:

- Domestic abuse: A single incident or pattern of abusive behaviour within a household. This may be between people in a relationship or between family members. These behaviours may be controlling, coercive, threatening, degrading, violent, sexually violent. For example, being refused food as punishment or being physically intimidated by a partner.

- Coercive control: A single incident or pattern of controlling behaviour. This can include manipulation, threats, humiliation, intimidation. The abuse can start small and increase over time. For example, at the beginning of a relationship, the abuser convinces their victim to cancel plans so they can spend time together. Over time, they cause issues with the people in their victim's support network. They tell their partner they have to choose them and end the other relationships. Eventually they isolate the victim completely.

- Harassment: Unwanted offensive or intimidating behaviour. For example, someone wants to begin a relationship with the person they like. When they ask them out the person says no, but they won't take no for an answer. Or, after a relationship ends, one person cannot accept that it is over. They keep messaging their ex and sabotaging their future relationships.

- Sexual exploitation AKA Sexploitation: Someone abuses their power over someone else (a child / a vulnerable person / someone they have private information about) to sexually abuse them. This may involve grooming the victim – gaining their trust, giving them gifts, showering them with affection etc. for sexual gratification or financial gain. For example, a 15-year-old is in a relationship with someone a few years older. They exchange nudes and think they are private. In reality, their partner has sold them online.

Ask students to look back at the case-study cards and identify which category each might fit into.

Task: Discuss and record different things which might happen early on in a relationship and could be a red flag, e.g., jealousy, gaslighting and aggressiveness.

Reflection

- What motivates these behaviours?

- How can I avoid these behaviours myself?

- How can I respond to these behaviours in a future partner?

- What help and support is available?

7 Issues with Porn and Sex Online

Sex Online

It is unsurprising that, as more of our lives have moved online, so too has sex. For generations who have grown up with smartphones, so much of the way they communicate, connect with each other and experiment is online. Teachers and parents can find it difficult to relate to this, but we will be most effective in empowering young people if we meet them where they are. It is acutely important to keep up with current trends in this rapidly evolving area and to ensure that the evidence you present is reliable and current.

Pornography

Porn is nothing new but there has been a rapid shift in the way it is consumed. Concerns are growing about the potential impact of this on the viewer and society more broadly.

When delivering lessons on porn, many of the same principles apply:

- Adopt a non-judgemental approach.
- Ensure what you are saying is supported by evidence.
- Avoid sensationalism.
- Acknowledge and accommodate the range of views, preferences and levels of experience there is likely to be in any classroom.
- Avoid heteronormative assumptions.
- Acknowledge gendered aspects without stereotyping.
- Empower students with critical thinking skills and self-awareness.
- Ensure your approach is age and stage appropriate by tailoring your curriculum to the level of knowledge and need for each class (see Chapter 1).

DOI: 10.4324/9781003437932-8

No Judgement

Whilst much of what we discuss in these lessons will highlight potential issues with porn, it is not our place to condemn porn or those who choose to watch it. The majority of students will access porn at some point. Acknowledging this is an important way to avoid creating any sense of shame or judgement.

This point can be made explicit by acknowledging that:

- Porn has existed for millennia in some form across different times and cultures.

- Today, lots of people choose to watch porn. Twenty-six million individuals in the UK viewed adult material in September 2020 (Waterson, 2019).

- According to PornHub's own research (2022), 36% of all viewers are female.

- Many people feel that porn is a healthy part of their sex lives – on their own and/or with a partner.

Setting the tone in this way is likely to engage students more fully in your lessons and have greater impact as an empowering, rather than prescriptive or judgemental, approach. In addition to this, remind students that:

- Some people watch porn every day and don't think it's a problem.

- Some people watch porn every day and are concerned they have a problem.

- Some people watch porn from time to time and don't think it's a problem.

- Some people watch porn with their partner and they both enjoy this.

- Some people would be outraged if their partner watched porn.

- Some people are disgusted by porn.

- Some people are curious about porn.

- Some people never watch porn.

Remind them to think about what these lessons mean for them personally whilst acknowledging that their future experiences and views may evolve.

Is Porn a Problem?

It's difficult to say. Some studies have concluded that porn has no adverse effects. Some have highlighted potentially positive effects, such as affirmation of sexual identity and enhanced sexual satisfaction. Others have highlighted potentially negative effects such as increased sexually violent behaviour and lower partnered sexual satisfaction (Grubbs, 2021).

The contradictory evidence:

- In a meta-analysis of studies from the 1980s to 2008, Malamuth (2009) found that porn did not cause most men to view women differently. However, men with pre-existing sexist attitudes or sexually violent behaviour seemed to have this propensity exacerbated (Hald & Yuen, 2009).

- Another meta-analysis of more than fifty studies found strong evidence to suggest that porn consumption is linked to lower sexual satisfaction for men in relationships (Wright et al., 2017). However, other studies have indicated that this may be the result of other factors like religious condemnation of porn, rather than porn itself (Perry, 2020).

- Porn has been shown to have the benefit of promoting greater sexual novelty and variety in couples (Miller et al., 2019) and to lead to greater sexual closeness (Kohut et al., 2018). Yet a further study found that watching porn reduces relational sex for heterosexual men. On the other hand, the opposite is true for gay men in relationships (Vaillancourt-Morel et al., 2020).

- Further studies have found a link in porn use and increased sexual objectification, greater levels of infidelity and greater relationship instability (Grubbs et al., 2019).

A NOTE ON... Porn Addiction

There is still some debate about this. Whilst some studies have shown brain states of compulsive porn users as being congruent with addiction, (Gola et al., 2016), other studies have disputed this, arguing that compulsion to watch porn is one manifestation of a broader hyper-sexuality (Steele et al., 2013).

When discussing this with students, it is important to stick to the facts. However, whilst the jury is still out on whether porn is addictive, the following can still be highlighted:

- Watching porn produces dopamine. Dopamine is the chemical produced in the reward centre of the brain and linked to addiction. There is speculation that users of porn may, over time, watch more graphic content to get the same rush of dopamine and that this may form a habitual cycle. This has been compared to gambling addiction.

- Some porn users have found their use has escalated to the point that they feel unable to control the urge to watch it. This can damage their relationships, ability to have and enjoy sex and their lives more broadly.

- Some people find the term 'porn addict' to be a useful description of their own experiences. This may help them to understand why they feel they have no control over their consumption and why they keep consuming porn even though it may be damaging their lives.

- Some people who describe themselves as sex addicts believe their addiction began with porn.

The point here is that it is difficult to say anything with certainty about the impact of porn. It is, therefore, important to:

- Present the nuance.

- Avoid being selective in which evidence is shared.

- Discuss 'potential' issues with porn.

Research on adolescents has also yielded conflicting conclusions, with one review of the existing literature concluding "although there are certainly links between pornography use and concerning outcomes in adolescence, it remains undetermined whether such associations are common and whether positive effects might also occur" (Grubbs & Krauss, 2021).

However, there is a huge body of evidence which indicates that the rapidly evolving picture for young people and their exposure to porn is cause for concern. Concerns include:

- Potential upset and confusion from early exposure.

- Normalisation of sexual violence, particularly towards women.

- Entrenching of misogynistic attitudes.

- Young people mimicking what they see, including sexual violence and coercion.

- Habitual, compulsive consumption.

- Unrealistic expectations about sex.

- Feelings of inadequacy and performance anxiety.

- Pleasure from real sex diminished.

- Jealousy or feelings of exclusion in relationships.

Chapter 5 discussed prevalence of child-on-child sexual abuse in schools and sexual violence more broadly. Many people would regard porn to be a contributing factor to rape culture which fuels much of the aspirational misogyny we are seeing in young men and on social media. As the report from the Children's Commissioner (2023) demonstrated, young people are not only watching porn which depicts degrading and violent acts towards women, many of them believe that this is what women want from sex.

Whilst it is likely that, just as with adults, the impact on young people will vary, it is crucial that we address these legitimate concerns through RSE. Sensationalising concerns about porn is unhelpful, but so is ignoring them. Even when the long-awaited Online Safety Bill comes into force, it is unlikely that porn will simply disappear from children's lives. As Natasha Devon, leading expert on children's mental health says: 'any of us who have a role in the lives of teenagers need to engage with this issue to make a difference. This is true especially of pornography. That means having some very difficult, very awkward conversations. The alternative, though, is worse' (Devon, 2023).

Early Exposure

Children are watching porn.

A 2023 report by the Children's Commissioner drew together research from focus groups with teenagers aged 13-19 and a survey of 1,000 young people aged 16-21. Of the 64% who said that they had ever seen online porn:

- The average age of first exposure to porn is 13. Ten percent of children had seen porn by age nine and 27% by age 11.

- Seventy-nine percent had encountered violent pornography before the age of 18.

- Forty-seven percent of young people aged between 16 and 21 believed that girls "expect" physical aggression in sex, and 42% said they believed most girls "enjoy" acts of sexual aggression.

- Fifty-eight percent of 16- to 21-year-old males and 42% of females said they had intentionally sought out online porn.

- Sixty-five percent had seen violence towards women in porn and 29% had seen violence towards men.

- Thirty-five percent of young adults had intentionally sought out violent pornography involving at least one act of sexual violence.

A NOTE ON... **The Law**

- A child is not breaking the law if they watch, or are in possession of pornographic material.

- Nude/ sexual photographs of people under the age of 18 are illegal to possess or distribute.

- Some extreme adult porn is illegal to watch including that which features:

  - A person's life being threatened.

  - A person's anus, breasts or genitalia likely to suffer serious or permanent injury.

  - Necrophilia (sex with dead bodies).

  - Bestiality (sex with animals).

- The government has developed a new Online Safety Bill aimed at regulating various parts of the internet. At the time of writing, this bill has not come into effect. Among other things, the draft bill proposes to make social-media companies legally responsible for protecting children online by:

  - Removing illegal content quickly.

  - Preventing children from accessing harmful content.

  - Enforcing age limits and age-checking measures.

  - Providing parents and children with clear and accessible ways to report problems online.

(Department for Science, Innovation and Technology and Department for Digital, Culture, Media & Sport, 2022).

What Are Children Watching?

Pornhub, the most popular porn site and a go-to for teen consumers, had the following featured on its home page on January 18, 2024:

- No age verification.

- Hardcore images.

- Links to local sex.

- Incest (more than half of the featured videos).

- Very young looking woman gagging.

- Petite Emma gets tiny ass stretched out.

- Anal, orgies, spanking, slut, squirting, teen pussy, butt plug, dildo, cream pie, light skinned girls, Latina, deep penetration, Thai teen, cuckold, submissive maid, slutty student.

When viewed through the lens of a child consumer, the list above is shocking. With one in four young people (23%) receiving no RSE from parents and carers and only one in six (17%) having regular discussions with parents and carers about RSE (Sex Ed Forum (b), 2022) many children are navigating porn without guidance. If the first sex education young people receive is from porn, their ideas about sex may be moulded by this.

A NOTE ON... **Ethical Porn**

There have been some attempts to create porn which avoids some of the problematic issues associated with a lot of mainstream content.
This is referred to as ethical porn / erotica / feminist porn / fair trade porn. Features vary but can include:

- Fair pay for the porn stars and an emphasis on consent in the filming process.

- Intimate, realistic sex acts, often based on mutual pleasure.

- Female directors.

- An emphasis on female sexual pleasure (moving away from the male gaze).

- Greater body diversity.

- Unlike a lot of porn out there, it is usually not free.

TEACHER TOOLKIT

Beginning the Conversation with Younger Students

There may be some students who have had no engagement with porn and be shocked by the concept. We do know, however, that many students will have watched porn before they reach you in Year 7 and those that have may have discussed this with their peers. It is, therefore, important that these lessons begin early so that young people begin to acquire the life skills to respond to this reality.

Task 1: Gauge where the class is at by completing the Good Sex / Bad Sex activity from Chapter 1. This will give you a good insight into the range of knowledge in the class and will help you to tailor your initial responses accordingly. Explain to students the aims and ethos of the RSE they'll be doing throughout their time at school, e.g., empowering, no judgement, fulfilling relationships.

Task 2: Group discussion – 'The internet is a good thing!' Do you agree? Record arguments for and against, e.g., Good – access to knowledge, communication, travel, etc.; Bad – exploitation, crime, illegal porn, etc. Have a class discussion and guide them to focus on the role of the internet in sex and relationships. Record a new list (neither good nor bad), e.g., online dating, long-distance relationships, porn, sending nudes. Ask groups to discuss what the pros and cons of each might be. Get some feedback as a class and narrow the focus to porn.

Task 3: Ask groups to discuss and record their answers to the following:

1. What is porn?

2. Has porn changed in recent years?

3. What is the law around porn?

4. Why do some people choose to watch porn?

5. What potential issues might there be with this?

Ask for feedback and pick up on the following points in response to each question:

1. Porn is images or videos of people naked and/or doing something sexual.

2. Easier access, younger exposure, extreme content, etc.

3. It is not illegal for young people to watch porn, but certain kinds of porn are illegal, e.g., if it features anyone under the age of 18 or contains certain dangerous or violent acts.

4. Curiosity, sexual desire, masturbation, because their friends do, by accident, boredom, shown by someone else. Make the point that some people enjoy porn and don't see it as a problem but other people have many concerns about it.

5. Ask for their feedback and prompt further thinking with the following questions: What do they think about children being exposed? Is porn a good source of sex education? What impact might it have on the viewer? Etc.

TEACHER TOOLKIT

Lessons for Older Students

A Brief History of Porn

It is interesting to note that wherever we find human civilisations we tend to find porn.

- Pornography = representation of sexual behaviour in books, pictures, statues, films, and other media that is intended to cause sexual excitement. The word *pornography*, derived from the Greek *porni* ('prostitute') and *graphein* ('to write'), was originally defined as any work of art or literature depicting the life of prostitutes.

- However, porn predates the Ancient Greeks... cave drawings of genitals have been discovered in France and date back approximately 37,000 years.

- Archaeologists in Germany have discovered a 35,000 year-old ivory figurine of a women with hugely exaggerated breasts.

- The Indian *Kama Sutra*, dating back as far as 400 BCE, is a graphic guide to sexual positions and sexual pleasure.

- Swedish cave drawings of people having sex have been dated back to 1000 BCE.

- Nepalese statues from approx. 400 CE depict graphic sex acts.

- The medieval Spanish church San Pedro de Cervatos features detailed cornices which with human figurines masturbating and having sex.

- In more recent history, *Le Coucher de la Mariée* (1896) was the first porn film.

- Pornographic photography became very popular in the Victorian era.

- By the 1920s, penny peep-show machines became popular, showing short pornographic films.

- In the 1960s, as sexual attitudes were becoming more liberal, porn magazines, most famously *Playboy* took off.

- By the late 1970s, the majority of videotape sales were pornographic.

- Porn became huge business and, by the 1990s, porn stars were earning huge sums of money. Increasingly, extreme bodies and plastic surgery became intertwined with the porn industry. Magazines and videos could be more easily purchased, and consumers had a greater variety to choose from.

- Porn was big business, but by the time the internet entered people's homes in the late 1990s, the industry began to lose its grip. Today, big sites like Pornhub give most of their content away for free.

Discussion - Where Are We Now and What Has Changed?

The internet changed so much about porn consumption: explicit, often extreme and even illegal content can now be accessed by anyone, anywhere, as often as they like.

Whilst many people see this as a good thing, there are others who have raised serious concerns about the impact this is having.

Linking to Self-Esteem and Body Image

- The average age of first exposure to porn is 13. Ten percent of children had seen porn by age nine and 27% by age 11 (2023 report by the Children's Commissioner).

- Studies have indicated that:

  - Watching porn may have an impact on sexual behaviour. Younger viewers are most likely to try to copy what they see.

- ○ Watching porn can increase the likelihood of seeing sex as purely physical and devoid of emotion.

- ○ Watching porn can have a negative impact on self-esteem and body image.

Group Discussion

- What do they think should be the minimum age at which people first watch porn?

- Should young people try to protect themselves from porn? How might they do this if so? What boundaries might be useful?

- What do they think about the current laws? Would they change anything?

- Is it okay for someone to show someone else porn? (Pick up on privacy, consent, age, peer pressure.)

- Are there healthier/safer ways for people to watch porn if they choose to? (E.g., more mature, had a good foundation of sex education, in private, ensuring the content is compatible with their values.)

Fantasy vs Reality

Helping students to understand the difference between sex in porn and sex in real life helps them to develop their critical thinking skills and to contextualise content they may have engaged with or been exposed to.

Begin by sharing the following true account:

In 2015, Ryan Stone, a 30-year-old man from Colorado in the US, was sentenced to 160 years in prison after trying to bring Grand Theft Auto (GTA) to life. Stone, believed to be a keen gamer and fan of GTA, went on a rampage which included carjacking several cars (one of which had a baby in it), triggering a high-speed police chase across five counties and, finally, running over a police officer. He later claimed that he hoped the notoriety gained would earn him advertising money from YouTube.

Discussion Questions

- Is this the average response to playing a game like GTA?

- Why not?

Tease out the fact that most people are able to distinguish between fantasy and reality and not try to bring the fantasy to life (if that fantasy is dangerous and damaging).

Draw the parallel with porn:

- Porn is a fantasy version of sex.

- Porn will often feature more extreme fantasies.

- Understanding the difference between porn and real sex is an important key to tipping the 'Good Sex / Bad Sex' scales in the right direction.

- If people got all their sex education from porn, what impression would they get?

Task

Ask groups to create tables comparing sex in porn with sex in real life. Discuss as a class and unpack any misconceptions, e.g.:

Sex in Porn	Sex in Real Life
Often focuses on male pleasure only	Can involve so much more than that
Extreme bodies, e.g., very large penises, boob jobs	A whole range
Sex lasts a long time	Average time for penis-in-vagina penetration is around four minutes
Consent rarely featured	Consent negotiated from the start and throughout
Contraception rarely featured or discussed	Contraception important and everyone's responsibility
Rough sex normalised	Many of the acts would be very painful and undesirable for many
Degrading acts normalised	Many people would be offended
Women's bodies treated like objects	Sexual agency and mutual pleasure is important for most people
Anal sex normalised and done in ways that can be dangerous	Anal sex is a minority sex act, and there are safer ways of doing it
Transactional	Intimate

And so on. Unpack what might be problematic if people think the porn version represents reality and try to mimic this.

Porn and Good Sex / Bad Sex

Helping students to develop their sense of self and agency around sex is a key component in empowering them to avoid some of the potential problems associated with porn. Building on previous learning, this activity helps students reflect personally on what this means for them in practice.

Look back to the 'Good Sex / Bad Sex' posters.

Class discussion: How might porn contribute to tipping the scales in the wrong direction? What can be done to tip the scales in the right direction (including if people choose to watch porn)?

Case Studies – Group Task

Read through each case study and discuss:

- What is going on here?

- What short-term impact might this have?

- What long-term impact might this have?

- How is this affecting each person's balance on the good sex / bad sex scales?

- What can each person do to empower themselves to tip the 'Good Sex / Bad Sex' scales in the right direction?

Maxine (17) has been watching porn since she was in junior school. Now she is in a real sexual relationship she finds herself trying to perform like a porn star. She feels disassociated from herself and her partner. Although she can orgasm alone, she has never done so with someone else. When her partner has tried, she's found it awkward and just tried to impress them instead. She's starting to feel like her early exposure to porn has left her feeling empty and detached when it comes to sex, and this makes her really sad.	Sophie (18) has watched porn a few times but isn't really bothered by it. Her new boyfriend says he doesn't watch porn but he keeps asking her to do things which indicate this may not be true. He has been putting pressure on her to try anal sex even though she's said she doesn't want to. Last week, he ejaculated in her face without asking and last time they had sex, he put his hand around her throat. She feels embarrassed and ashamed and doesn't know what to do.

Tom (16) started watching porn as soon as the urge to masturbate kicked in. Since then, he has watched porn every time he's masturbated. Recently, his phone broke so he couldn't access porn. When he tried to masturbate, he found he couldn't sustain an erection. Now he's worried about what will happen when he has real sex.	Sam (11) is allowed his device in his room at all times with no parental restrictions. He recently discovered porn and though he doesn't find it sexually arousing he can't stop watching it. He has been looking at more-and-more extreme content and feels he can't stop himself. He's started having nightmares about violent sex acts and he's worried about the impact this is having on him.
Harry (19) has always watched porn and doesn't see an issue with it. He's been hooking up with lots of older men who say they like him because he's a twink (looks young and attractive). He likes the effect he has on older men and has always been happy having casual sex. Mostly, the sex is with strangers and often they don't speak to each other or make eye contact. Recently, he hooked up with Guy from uni who he's fancied for ages. The sex was completely different – it was intimate and affectionate and emotional. Guy's asked Harry if they can be exclusive, but Harry's worried he won't be satisfied without risky sex with strangers.	Steph (18) watched a bit of porn when she was younger but isn't particularly interested in it. When she did watch it, she was surprised to discover that other people's vulvas looked different to hers. She started to feel that her vulva was weird and unattractive and put off having sex until recently. At first, she insisted on keeping covered and having the light off. Over time, she opened up to her partner who assured her that her vulva is completely normal and beautiful. Despite this, she cannot get over the feeling of insecurity. As a result, rather than being in the moment, she is detached and self-conscious. This is becoming a barrier to pleasure and intimacy for her and her partner.

Opinion Continuum

Ask students to stand at the back of the class. As each statement is read out, they should physically position themselves according to where their opinion fits. Ask volunteers to justify their response to each statement and allow for discussion.

- Children should never be exposed to porn.
- The government has no right to interfere with who watches porn or what they watch.
- Porn is a good source of sex education.
- Porn ruins real sex.

- Porn damages relationships.

- Porn causes sexual violence.

- Porn makes people feel insecure.

- All porn should be legal.

- Porn is addictive.

- The world would be better without porn.

Self-Generated Content

Increasingly, porn is moving away from the industry towards self-generated content. Young people are often attracted to this as a way of making money and may feel that this is an empowered choice. RSE lessons are a useful opportunity for young people to explore this whilst developing an idea of some of the potential issues and ultimately making informed decisions which are right for them. By exploring this in a non-judgemental way, young people will be better placed to make empowered decisions and to be vigilant to exploitation and other risks.

What's the debate?

With over two million content creators and an annual net revenue of $2.5 billion (Primack, 2021), OnlyFans is the most successful platform for creators to monetise their content.

Some people have argued that this is a positive shift which empowers both the creator and the consumer. Creators describe having greater autonomy over their content and those with large followings can make huge sums of money. Blac Chyna, one of the most successful creators, made over $20 million in a year from her content (Baio, 2023).

Increasingly, consumers are willing to pay a monthly fee for content which matches their tastes rather than having to scroll through free sites. The 420 million active monthly users (Baio, 2023) are drawn to the personalised and intimate engagement they can have with the creators and will often pay cash tips for increased interaction.

Some people have also praised the way in which OnlyFans has subverted the narrow beauty standards perpetuated by Hollywood porn studios which pushed a singular aesthetic (e.g., large breasts and no pubic hair), exploited its stars and reinforced misogyny. Creators on OnlyFans represent greater diversity which more accurately reflects the real world.

However, although OnlyFans promotes itself as an empowering platform which has paid out more than $10 billion to its creators (Biino M, 2023), it is not without controversy.

OnlyFans has come under criticism for failing to adequately remove child pornography shared on the site. They have also been accused of discriminating against sex workers, allowing creators to mislead consumers and creating the illusion of safety whilst exploiting and pimping out the creators. Many people have challenged the idea that OnlyFans empowers creators, instead accusing it of reinforcing misogyny and the pornification of women's bodies.

Many young people find the prospect of making quick, easy money appealing. As sites like OnlyFans continue to grow, many are concerned that young people who become creators will come to regret this later. The 2020 BBC Three documentary *Nudes4Sale* gives an insight into why young people are attracted to becoming creators and what this experience is like. The film makers also discovered under 18s finding ways to sell their content despite the age verification process. A BBC investigation revealed that abusers use multiple platforms to sexually exploit young people by profiteering from their content (De Gallier, 2020).

TEACHER TOOLKIT

Self-Generated Content

Introduce the topic and explain that as this industry grows, a debate has emerged about whether this is a good or bad thing.

Ask pairs to discuss and record the potential pros and cons, including for the creator and the consumer. Prompt them to think about things like consent, autonomy, privacy, personal boundaries, longer term considerations, etc. Ask for feedback as a class.

Share the following statement: "OnlyFans creators are empowered." Ask pairs to decide if they agree or disagree and to write a brief statement justifying their position. Create an opinion continuum along the back of the classroom wall and ask pairs to position themselves accordingly – strongly agree at one end, strongly disagree at the other. Pairs can split up if they are in disagreement. Get a discussion going and allow statements to be read out by those who want to. Do not guide; allow students to go back and forth between divergent views. Finally, ask students if they would like to change their position on the continuum and, if so, what has changed their mind. Finish by reminding students that the divergence of views in the classroom is likely to be reflected in society. Remind them that your mission is to empower them to go off into their lives and make decisions about sex and relationships which tip the scales in the right direction for them (see the 'Good Sex / Bad Sex' activity from Chapter 1).

Nudes

The 2021 Ofsted Review into Sexual Abuse in Schools and Colleges revealed the proliferation of nudes being exchanged between young people, both solicited and unsolicited. Whilst children of any gender can be harassed and abused online, the report confirmed existing research which demonstrates that girls are disproportionately targeted. Girls reported:

- Being sent pictures or videos they did not want to see (88%).

- Being put under pressure to provide sexual images of themselves (80%).

- Having pictures or videos that they sent being shared more widely without their knowledge or consent (73%).

- Being photographed or videoed without their knowledge or consent (59%).

- Having pictures or videos of themselves that they did not know about being circulated (51%).

Helping students find a path through this can be a difficult balancing act. On the one hand, sharing of nudes may, ultimately form part of an empowered approach to their sex lives. On the other, the potential for disempowerment, embarrassment, legal issues, harassment, abuse and exploitation is huge. As always, lecturing students about what they should / should not do is likely to be ineffective. Instead, naming the nuance, building their skills and empowering them to work things out for themselves will lay the foundations for now and the future. Any lessons on this subject will be most impactful when delivered in the context of healthy relationships (see Chapter 6).

TEACHER TOOLKIT

For Younger Students

Laying the Foundations

Intro: Our online life is not just something that happens to us. Throughout our lives we make choices about what we share, who we share things with, what data we share, which apps and platforms we engage with and so on. In many ways, we curate the version of ourselves we want to share with the world.

Task: Ask students to sketch out two hypothetical scenarios:

Person 1 has carefully curated an online life which they feel benefits them personally and professionally (e.g., strong privacy settings, positive posts, connecting with friends and family abroad, limited time engaging, effectively using LinkedIn, etc. to build a professional presence, etc.).

Person 2 has not set any boundaries and now their online persona is damaging their real life (no privacy settings, embarrassing photos, inappropriate posts, nudes shared, etc.).

Discussion

What impact might each scenario have on their lives?

Who feels more empowered?

What strategies can each of us use to ensure an empowered approach to life online?

Online Health Check

Ask students to independently respond to the following questions.

Are you aware of who has your data? For example, how many things you are signed up to with your email address?
Do you have any social-media profiles? Which?
Do you have strong privacy settings across all platforms, i.e., only friends can see your content?
Do you only accept friend requests from (or followers who are) people you know?

| What impression would someone get of you from your profiles? (Think all the way back to when you first started posting.) |
| Would you be happy for anyone (e.g., your parents / grandparents / teachers / future employers) to see everything you've posted online, including in PMs and group chats? |
| Do you feel empowered in how you are engaging in all aspects of your life online? |
| Would you benefit from putting any additional boundaries in place? |
| What would you do if something went wrong? |

Share Some Top Tips

- Regularly check your privacy settings across all apps. It is safest to have a private profile and only allow friends to view your content. It is also safest to turn off location settings so people can't monitor where you are.

- Social-media sites allow you to block and report unwanted contact. Use this feature if you need to.

- Do a thorough health check at home and remove any content you're not happy with.

- Be careful about what you post, even between friends. Chats may feel private but often they are not. Try to ensure that what you say/share reflects your true character. If you are in a group chat where people are crossing the line, think about leaving.

Building on Prior Learning

Nudes

Begin with a private reflection on values. Ask students to silently and privately record their responses to the following:

(1) What's your general opinion on people sharing nudes?

(2) How do you feel about people pressuring others to send nudes?

(3) What kinds of things does someone say if they're trying to pressure someone else into sending a nude?

(4) What kinds of things could someone say if they don't want to send a nude?

(5) Would you ever pressure someone else into sending you a nude?

(6) How would you feel if someone you fancy / are in a relationship with is pressuring you to send a nude but you don't want to? What do you think you could do in this situation to remain empowered?

(7) Is it okay to send someone a nude without asking their permission? What kinds of things could someone say to make sure they have consent to share a nude? What kind of responses would they need to have to know they have consent?

(8) Do you, personally have any 'red lines' when it comes to nudes?

(9) What are your personal goals for how you want to navigate nudes and online sex more generally?

(10) How will you ensure that your behaviours match your personal goals and values?

Ask for some non-personal discussion of Questions 3, 4 and 7. Allow students to add notes to their personal reflection if desired.

Share the statistics from the Ofsted report with students.

Class discussion: Does this picture reflect their perception of what's happening in schools?

Group Work – Discuss and Brainstorm

Why do people send nudes?

Feedback as a class: Discuss which reasons might be based in empowerment (e.g., trusting relationship, both people sexually fulfilled) and those which might not (e.g., feeling under pressure, not thinking about the consequences).

Group work – discuss and brainstorm:

What are some of the potential short- and long-term issues which can arise from sending nudes?

Feedback as a class: Pick up on the loss of privacy and control over the content, exploitation, relationship breakdowns, betrayal of trust, digital footprint, etc.

Case Studies

Vince (18) recently found out that a video of him masturbating had made its way to loads of gay porn sites. When he was younger, he did a live web stream on a porn site. It hadn't occurred to him that this would be recorded. He discovered this when he ran his face through facial recognition software and discovered the video on multiple sites around the world. He's been trying to get it taken down ever since, but as soon as it goes from one place it pops up somewhere else.	Millie (14) has been seeing her boyfriend for a few months and he has been asking for some nudes. She really likes him and wants to make him happy, but she doesn't want to take the risk. Her boyfriend keeps putting pressure on her and sending her pictures of himself. She's starting to worry that he'll dump her if she doesn't give in. One night, she takes a load of photos on her phone but decides not to send them. Her parents discover the photos, and they are not happy.
Si (15) has been chatting to people online and some of the chat has been getting sexual. He's bored and horny and looks forward to these chats. One of the people he's chatting to offers to transfer him £50 for a nude. He agrees and sends one without his face in it. They then offer him £100 for a full picture, including his face.	Carmen (19) had been with her partner for six months before they split up. Sometimes they would video them having sex. They both agreed to this, and both liked it. Now they've split up, Carmen still has the videos. She is angry and heartbroken that her ex has moved on with someone else. She decides to take revenge on her ex by uploading the video to a porn site and sending the link to his boss and family.

Ask Groups to Discuss Each Case Study

What went wrong?

Where has consent been violated?

How are they feeling?

What might happen next?

How could things have been handled differently?

Feedback as a class:

Ask students if they are able to define online 'sexploitation.' Explain that this refers to a type of abuse where one person manipulates or tricks another into a sexually compromising situation, sometimes for financial gain, sometimes for sexual gratification. This can happen to anyone at any age, but children can be particularly vulnerable to this. Look back at the case studies. Is there any evidence of sexploitation?

Ask pairs to then write their own case studies featuring sexploitation. These should include:

- Information about the victim. What's going on for them? How have they found themselves in this situation?

- Detail what has happened. You may need to give some prompts, e.g., grooming, coercion, sharing images and blackmail.

- Explain the outcome of the situation.

Ask students to group themselves into two sets of pairs. They should swap case studies and record notes on the following:

- Is there anything the victim could have done to protect themselves from this happening?

- What advice would you give to the victim after this had happened? What can they do now?

Ask pairs to feedback to each other and see if they can add any other ideas. Get some feedback as a class. Emphasise that sexploitation is always the fault of the perpetrator and never the victim but that each of us must be vigilant and protect ourselves as far as possible.

Final Discussion

Not all nude sharing involves sexploitation. Some people enjoy this as part of their sex lives and do not see a problem with this.

Discuss

Why do some people regard sharing nudes as a good thing?
Is sharing nudes ever risk free? Pick up on: Although some mitigations can be put in place, e.g., no face in the picture, consent, trust, privacy measures, there may still be risks involved, e.g., a device is stolen or hacked, or a relationship breaks down.

A NOTE ON... Facial Recognition Software

This software now makes it possible to match a face and find it any-where on the World Wide Web. This has increased the risks around sending nudes and is something students should be aware of. For example, a young person, aged 18 or under, shares nudes or live streams sexual content of themselves. This is recorded and uploaded online, without their permission or knowledge. This child porn is illegally shared and downloaded and on some sites, is used to generate an illegal income for those selling the content. The young person has no idea about this until later when they / a friend/ a part-ner / an employer puts their photo through facial recognition software. Upon discovery of this, the victim informs the police and Interpol. They contact the websites. Some take down the content, some ignore the request. No matter what they do, the content keeps popping back up.

A NOTE ON... Revenge Porn

Section 33 of the Criminal Justice and Courts Act makes it illegal to share, without consent, private sexual photos and videos in England and Wales. The maximum sentence is two years in prison. In 2021, the Domestic Abuse Act was amended to include the offence of threatening to share such material.

A NOTE ON... Artificial Intelligence (AI)

As user engagement with AI increases, there is no doubt that this rapidly emerging technology will intersect with the world of porn. It will be important for teachers to keep abreast of these developments and continue to give students the knowledge and skills to navigate this.

REFERENCES

Amnesty International, 2018. Available at: https://www.amnesty.org/en/latest/news/2018/10/its-intersex-awareness-day-here-are-5-myths-we-need-to-shatter/ (Accessed 9 February 2023)

Baio, A., 2023. OnlyFans' top earners bring in these astonishing amounts. *Indie 100*, 5 April. Available at: https://www.indy100.com/viral/onlyfans-top-earners-amount-2659741964 (Accessed 24 August 2023)

Bates, L., 2021. *Men who hate women: From incels to pickup artists: The truth about extreme misogyny and how it affects us all.* Sourcebooks, Inc.

Bates, L., 2022. *Fix the system, not the women.* Simon and Schuster.

BBC News, 2021. *Maya Forstater: Woman wins tribunal appeal over transgender tweets.* Available at: https://www.bbc.co.uk/news/uk-57426579 (Accessed 23 August 2023)

BBC News, 2022. *Hate crimes recorded by police up by more than a quarter.* Available at: https://www.bbc.co.uk/news/uk-63157965 (Accessed 12 December, 2022)

Biino, M., 2023. How much money only fans creators make. *Business Insider*, 18 August. Available at: https://www.businessinsider.com/how-much-money-onlyfans-creators-make-real-examples-2023-1?r=US&IR=T (Accessed 23 July 2023)

Blue Seat Studios, 2015. *Tea consent (clean).* [Online Video], 23 December 2022. Available at: https://www.youtube.com/watch?v=fGoWLWS4-kU. (Accessed 13 May 2023)

British Medical Journal, no date. Doctors' reluctance to discuss anal sex is letting down young women. *Newsroom.* Available at: https://www.bmj.com/company/newsroom/doctors-reluctance-to-discuss-anal-sex-is-letting-down-young-women/ (Accessed 3 June 2023)

Children's Commissioner, 2023. *'A lot of it is actually just abuse' young people and pornography.* Available at: https://assets.childrenscommissioner.gov.uk/wpuploads/2023/02/cc-a-lot-of-it-is-actually-just-abuse-young-people-and-pornography-updated.pdf (Accessed 2 July 2023)

Cut, 2019. *100 People tell Us about their worst breakup.* Available at: https://www.youtube.com/watch?v=RfxU4GE4vWM (Accessed 9 April 2023)

Das, S., 2022. Inside the violent, misogynistic world of TikTok's new star, Andrew Tate. *The Guardian*, 6 August. Available at: https://www.theguardian.com/technology/2022/aug/06/andrew-tate-violent-misogynistic-world-of-tiktok-new-star (Accessed 23 August 2023)

De Gallier, T., 2020. The hidden danger of selling nudes online. *BBC Three*, 6 July. Available at: https://www.bbc.co.uk/bbcthree/article/5e7dad06-c48d-4509-b3e4-6a7a2783ce30 (Accessed 28 August 2023)

Department for Education, 2014. *The equality act 2010 and schools.* Available at: https:// assets.publishing.service.gov.uk/government/uploads/system/uploads/attachment _data/file/315587/Equality_Act_Advice_Final.pdf (Accessed 20 May 2023)

Department for Education, 2020. *Relationships education, relationships and sex education (RSE) and health education.* Available at: https://assets.publishing.service.gov.uk/ government/uploads/system/uploads/attachment_data/file/1090195/Relationships _Education_RSE_and_Health_Education.pdf (Accessed 13 May 2023)

Department for Education, 2023. *Keeping Children Safe in Education.* Available at: https:// assets.publishing.service.gov.uk/media/64f0a68ea78c5f000dc6f3b2/Keeping_ children_safe_in_education_2023.pdf (Accessed: 13 January 2024)

Department for Science, Innovation and Technology and Department for Digital, Culture, Media & Sport, 2022. *A guide to the online safety bill.* Available at: https://www.gov.uk/ guidance/a-guide-to-the-online-safety-bill (Accessed 6 June 2023)

Devon, N., 2023. Your child has almost certainly watched porn – Here's how to talk to them about it. *Evening Standard*, 2 February. Available at: https://www.standard.co.uk /comment/your-child-watched-porn-education-parents-talk-b1057423.html (Accessed 3 February 2023)

Dunne, S. A., 2017. *Rape in online spaces: An examination of rape culture on Twitter through the Steubenville rape case.* Available at: https://www.researchgate.net/publication /308174349_Rape_in_Online_Spaces_An_Examination_of_Rape_Culture_on_Twitter _through_the_Steubenville_Rape_Case (Accessed 28 August 2023)

Elsesser, K., 2023. Elon musk deems 'Cis' a Twitter slur–here's why it's is so polarizing. *Forbes*, 2 July. Available at: https://www.forbes.com/sites/kimelsesser/2023/07/02/ elon-musk-deems-cis-a-twitter-slurheres-why-its-is-so-polarizing/?sh=567c92594ac6 (Accessed 2 August 2023)

Equality Act 2010, c39. Available at: https://www.legislation.gov.uk/ukpga/2010/15/ contents (Accessed 23 August 2023)

Erens, B., et al., 2013. National survey of sexual attitudes and lifestyles 3 technical report. *National Surveys of Sexual Attitudes and Lifestyles.* Available at: https://www.natsal.ac .uk/natsal-survey/natsal-3 (Accessed 2 August 2023)

Farrer & Co., 2022. *Addressing child-on-child abuse: A resource for schools and colleges.* Available at: https://www.farrer.co.uk/globalassets/clients-and-sectors/safeguarding/ addressing-child-on-child-abuse.pdf (Accessed 20 June 2023)

Femicide Census, 2020. *Femicide census 2020.* Available at: https://www.femicidecensus .org/wp-content/uploads/2022/02/010998-2020-Femicide-Report_V2.pdf (Accessed 3 June 2023)

Frederick, D. A., John, H. K. S., Garcia, J. R. and Lloyd, E. A., 2018. Differences in orgasm frequency among gay, lesbian, bisexual, and heterosexual men and women in a U.S. National sample. Archives of Sexual Behavior, 47(1), 273–288. doi: 10.1007/s10508-017- 0939-z. Epub 2017 Feb 17. PMID: 28213723 (Accessed 21 August 2023)

Gola, M., Lewczuk, K. and Skorko, M., 2016. What matters: Quantity or quality of pornography use? Psychological and behavioral factors of seeking treatment for problematic pornography use. *The Journal of Sexual Medicine*, 13(5), 815–824.

Goldfarb, E. S. and Lieberman, L. D., 2021. Three decades of research: The case for comprehensive sex education. *Journal of Adolescent Health*, 68, 13–27. Available at: https://doi.org/10.1016/j.jadohealth.2020.07.036 (Accessed 20 June 2023)

Goldstein, E. S., 2018. Anal sex practices: How do gay men and straight women compare? *Bespoke Surgical.* Available at: https://bespokesurgical.com/2018/02/05/anal-sex-prep -practices-gay-men-straight-women-compare-2/ (Accessed 2 August 2023)

Grubbs, J. B. and Kraus, S. W., 2021. Pornography use and psychological science: A call for consideration. *Current Directions in Psychological Science*, 30(1), 68–75.

Grubbs, J. B., Wright, P. J., Braden, A. L., Wilt, J. A. and Kraus, S. W., 2019. Internet pornography use and sexual motivation: A systematic review and integration. *Annals of the International Communication Association*, 43(2), 117–155. https://doi.org/10.1080 /23808985.2019.1584045

Hald, G. M., Malamuth, N. M. and Yuen, C., 2010. Pornography and attitudes supporting violence against women: Revisiting the relationship in nonexperimental studies. *Aggressive Behavior*, 36, 14–20. https://doi.org/10.1002/ab.20328

Hinsliff, G., 2022. The PM sees votes in a culture war over trans rights, but this issue must transcend party politics. *The Guardian*, 13 April. Available at: https://www.theguardian .com/commentisfree/2022/apr/13/local-elections-tories-culture-war-trans-rights -conversion-practices (Accessed 24 February 2023)

House of Commons Justice Committee, 2017. *Restorative justice*. Available at: https:// publications.parliament.uk/pa/cm201617/cmselect/cmjust/164/164.pdf (Accessed 19 July 2023)

Julian, V., 2020. New research on reporting of trans issues shows 400% increase in coverage and varying perceptions on broader editorial standards. *IPSO*, 2 December. Available at: https://www.ipso.co.uk/news-press-releases/press-releases/new-research-on-reporting -of-trans-issues-shows-400-increase-in-coverage-and-varying-perceptions-on-broader -editorial-standards/ (Accessed 19 July 2023)

Just Like Us, 2022. *Majority of teachers want more guidance on supporting trans pupils, new research finds*. Available at: https://www.justlikeus.org/blog/2022/02/28/teachers -want-guidance-support-transgender-pupils-research/ (Accessed 12 June 2022)

Kohut, T., Balzarini, R. N., Fisher, W. A. and Campbell, L., 2018. Pornography's associations with open sexual communication and relationship closeness vary as a function of dyadic patterns of pornography use within heterosexual relationships. *Journal of Social and Personal Relationships*, 35(4), 655–676. https://doi.org/10.1177/0265407517743096

Lederer, A. M., 2016. *A critical analysis of conflicting perspectives: The impact of exposing young people to graphic images of sexually transmitted infections in sexuality education* (Doctoral dissertation, Indiana University).

McWhirter, J., 2008. *A review of safety education: Principles for effective practice*. Royal Society for the Prevention of Accidents.

Miller, D. J., McBain, K. A., Li, W. W. and Raggatt, P. T. F., 2019. Pornography, preference for porn-like sex, masturbation, and men's sexual and relationship satisfaction. *Personal Relationships*, 26(1), 93–113. https://doi.org/10.1111/pere.12267

Mitchell, K. R., Mercer, C. H., Ploubidis, G. B., Jones, K. G., Datta, J., Field, N., Copas, A. J., Tanton, C., Erens, B., Sonnenberg, P. and Clifton, S., 2013. Sexual function in Britain: Findings from the third National Survey of Sexual Attitudes and Lifestyles (Natsal-3). *The Lancet*, 382(9907), 1817–1829.

More in Common, 2022. *Britons and gender identity*. Available at: https://www .moreincommon.org.uk/our-work/research/britons-and-gender-identity/ (Accessed 12 June 2022)

NSPCC, 2022. *Gillick competency and Fraser guidelines*. Available at: https://learning .nspcc.org.uk/child-protection-system/gillick-competence-fraser-guidelines (Accessed 8 August 2023)

Nudes4Sale, 2020. BBC one. Directed by Josh Reynolds. *BBC Three*, 6 May. Available at: https://www.bbc.co.uk/iplayer/episode/p087m1nh/nudes4sale (Accessed 28 August 2023)

Office for National Statistics, 2023. *Gender identity by age and sex, England and Wales: Census 2021*. Available at: https://www.ons.gov.uk/peoplepopulationandcommunity/ culturalidentity/genderidentity/articles/genderidentityageandsexenglandandwalesc ensus2021/2023-01-25 (Accessed 23 August 2023)

Ofsted, 2021. *Review of sexual abuse in schools and colleges*. Available at: https://www.gov
.uk/government/publications/review-of-sexual-abuse-in-schools-and-colleges/review-of
-sexual-abuse-in-schools-and-colleges (Accessed 14 May 2023)

Oppenheim, M., 2023. TikTok 'failing to act' as Andrew Tate videos still seen by children as
young as 13. *The Independent*, July 2023. Available at: https://www.independent.co.uk
/news/uk/home-news/andrew-tate-tristan-videos-tiktok-b2362496.html (Accessed 23
August 2023)

Perry, S. L., 2020. Is the link between pornography use and relational happiness really more
about masturbation? Results from two national surveys. *The Journal of Sex Research*,
57(1), 64–76.

Pornhub, 2022. *The 2022 year in review*. Available at: https://www.pornhub.com/insights
/2022-year-in-review (Accessed 3 June 2023)

Primack, D., 2021. OnlyFans has tons of users, but can't find investors. *Axios*, 19 August.
Available at: https://www.axios.com/2021/08/19/onlyfans-investors-struggle (Accessed
22 August 2023)

Rape Crisis England and Wales, no date. *Rape and sexual assault statistics*. Available
at: https://rapecrisis.org.uk/get-informed/statistics-sexual-violence/#:~:text=How
%20many%20women%20are%20raped%20or%20sexually%20assaulted%20every
%20year%3F&text=That's%201%20in%2030%20women,the%20year%20ending%2
0March%202022 (Accessed 14 May 2023)

Rape Crisis England and Wales, no date. *What is sexual harassment?* Available at https://
rapecrisis.org.uk/get-informed/types-of-sexual-violence/what-is-sexual-harassment/
(Accessed 3 June 2023)

Rape Crisis Scotland, 2021. *Briefing false allegations (2021)*. Available at: https://www
.rapecrisisscotland.org.uk/resources/False-allegations-briefing-2021.pdf (Accessed 3
June 2023)

Rigby, K., Brown, M., Anagnostou, P., Ross, M. W. and Rosser, B. R. S., 1989. Shock tactics to
counter AIDS: The Australian experience. *Psychology and Health*, 3(3), 145–159.

Sex Ed Forum, 2020. *RSE for disabled pupils and pupils with special educational needs*.
Available   at: https://www.sexeducationforum.org.uk/sites/default/files/field/
attachment/RSE%20for%20disabled%20pupils%20and%20pupils%20with%20SEN
%20-%20SEF.pdf (Accessed 2 April 2023)

Sex Ed Forum (a), 2022. *Relationships and sex education: The evidence*. Available at: https://
www.sexeducationforum.org.uk/sites/default/files/field/attachment/RSE%20The
%20Evidence%20-%20SEF%202022.pdf (Accessed 28 May 2023)

Sex Ed Forum (b), 2022. *Young people's RSE poll 2021*. Available at: https://www
.sexeducationforum.org.uk/sites/default/files/field/attachment/Young%20Peoples
%20RSE%20Poll%202021%20-%20SEF%201%20Feb%202022.pdf (Accessed 12 July
2023)

Sherwin, A., 2013. Serena Williams apologises after comment that rape victim 'shouldn't
have put herself in that position'. *The Independent*, 19 June. Available at: https://www
.independent.co.uk/news/people/news/serena-williams-apologises-after-comment-that
-rape-victim-shouldn-t-have-put-herself-in-that-position-8664998.html (Accessed 25
August 2023)

Steele, V. R., Staley, C., Fong, T. and Prause, N., 2013. Sexual desire, not hypersexuality,
is related to neurophysiological responses elicited by sexual images. *Socioaffective
neuroscience & Psychology*, 3(1), 20770.

Stonewall, 2017. *School report 2017*. Available at: https://www.stonewall.org.uk/school
-report-2017 (Accessed 23 August 2023)

Swinford, S., 2022. Teachers should not pander to trans pupils, says Suella Braverman. *The Times*, 27 May. Available at: https://www.thetimes.co.uk/article/teachers-should-not -pander-to-trans-pupils-says-suella-braverman-2qfgj70rv (Accessed 23 August 2023)

Unesco, 2018. *International technical guidance on sexuality education: An evidence-informed approach*. Available at: https://unesdoc.unesco.org/ark:/48223/pf0000260770 (Accessed 13 May 2023)

Vaillancourt-Morel, M.-P., Rosen, N. O., Willoughby, B. J., Leonhardt, N. D. and Bergeron, S., 2020. Pornography use and romantic relationships: A dyadic daily diary study. *Journal of Social and Personal Relationships*, 37(10–11), 2802–2821. https://doi.org/10.1177 /0265407520940048

Walker, P., 2023. Rishi Sunak accused of mocking trans people in joke to Tory MPs. *The Guardian*, 19 June. Available at: https://www.theguardian.com/politics/2023/jun/19/ rishi-sunak-accused-of-mocking-trans-people-in-joke-to-tory-mps (Accessed 23 August 2023)

Walsh, K., Zwi, K., Woolfenden, S. and Shlonsky, A., 2015. School-based education programmes for the prevention of child sexual abuse. *Cochrane Database of Systematic Reviews*, 4. Art. No.: CD004380. DOI: 10.1002/14651858.CD004380.pub3 (Accessed 25 August 2023)

Waterson, J., 2019. Half of adults in UK watched porn during pandemic, says Ofcom. *The Guardian*, 9 June. Available at: https://www.theguardian.com/media/2021/jun/09/half -british-adults-watched-porn-pandemic-ofcom (Accessed 2 July 2023)

Wilson, K. L., Wiley, D. C. and Rosen, B., 2012. Texas sexuality education instruction: Shame and fear-based methodology. *Journal of Health Education Teaching*, 3(1), 1–10.

World Health Organization, 2006. *Defining sexual health: Report of a technical consultation on sexual health, 28–31 January 2002*. World Health Organization.

World Health Organization, 2023. *Female genital mutilation*. Available at: https://www.who .int/news-room/fact-sheets/detail/female-genital-mutilation (Accessed 25 August 2023)

Wright, P. J., Tokunaga, R. S., Kraus, A. and Klann, E., 2017. Pornography consumption and satisfaction: A meta-analysis. *Human Communication Research*, 43(3), 315–343.

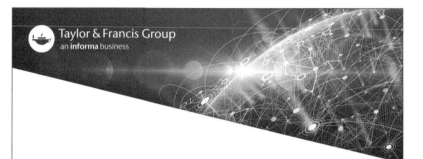